LEGITIMATION
AND INTEGRATION
IN DEVELOPING
SOCIETIES

Westview Replica Editions

The concept of Westview Replica Editions is a respose to the continuing crisis in academic and informational publishing. Library budgets for books have been severely curtailed. Ever larger portions of general library budgets are being diverted from the purchase of books and used for data banks, computers, micromedia, and other methods of information retrieval. Interlibrary loan structures further reduce the edition sizes required to satisfy the needs of the scholarly community. Economic pressures (particularly inflation and high interest rates) on the university presses and the few private scholarly publishing companies have severely limited the capacity of the industry to properly serve the academic and research communities. As a result, many manuscripts dealing with important subjects, often representing the highest level of scholarship, are no longer economically viable publishing projects—or, if accepted for publication, are typically subject to lead times ranging from one to three years.

Westview Replica Editions are our practical solution to the problem. We accept a manuscript in camera-ready form, typed according to our specifications, and move it immediately into the production process. As always, the selection criteria include the importance of the subject, the work's contribution to scholarship, and its insight, originality of thought, and excellence of exposition. The responsibility for editing and proofreading lies with the author or sponsoring institution. We prepare chapter headings and display pages, file for copyright, and obtain Library of Congress Cataloging in Publication Data. A detailed manual contains simple instructions for preparing the final typescript, and our editorial staff is always available to answer questions.

The end result is a book printed on acid-free paper and bound in sturdy library-quality soft covers. We manufacture these books ourselves using equipment that does not require a lengthy make-ready process and that allows us to publish first editions of 300 to 600 copies and to reprint even smaller quantities as needed. Thus, we can produce Replica Editions quickly and can keep even very specialized books in print as long as there is a demand for them.

About the Book and Author

Legitimation and Integration
in Developing Societies: The Case of India

Reuven Kahane

Though characterized by great human diversity and subject to economic constraints—typically disintegrative forces—Indian society has managed to function in a democratic manner through institutionalization of conflict among the myriad of competing ethnic, religious, and political factions. The author of this book maintains that the relative unity of Indian society can be explained by its unique pattern of integration, which allows conflicting forces to cooperate through mediatory institutions. Such institutions, he argues, link differing codes of behavior and equalize opposing groups, creating structures that serve as bridging mechanisms within the society. Dr. Kahane goes beyond the example of India, pointing to general theoretical considerations important for the analysis of political legitimation and integration in diverse societies. He suggests a model of society in which conflicts are accentuated for integrative purposes, illustrates the structure of the mechanisms by which antagonistic elements of society are connected, and stresses that analysis of the patterns in which social units (political, cultural, and religious) are linked is often the most efficient means of explaining the nature of a given social order.

Dr. Kahane is senior lecturer in the Department of Sociology and Social Anthropology at the Hebrew University of Jerusalem, and is a research scholar in the Modernization and Comparative Civilizations Unit at the University's Harry S. Truman Research Institute.

LEGITIMATION AND INTEGRATION IN DEVELOPING SOCIETIES
The Case of India

Reuven Kahane

Westview Press / Boulder, Colorado

The author would like to thank Harry S. Truman Research Institute for the Advancement of Peace, Hebrew University of Jerusalem, for their support in the publication of this book.

HN
6 83. 5
. K33

A Westview Replica Edition

Published in 1982 in the United States of America by
Westview Press, Inc.
5500 Central Avenue
Boulder, Colorado 80301
Frederick A. Praeger, President and Publisher

Library of Congress Catalog Card Number 82-51017
ISBN 0-86531-921-9

Printed and bound in the United States of America

CONTENTS

TABLES

PREFACE

In most Third World countries the emergence of nationhood has been accompanied by the rise of universalistic, egalitarian expectations. This process in turn has accentuated primordial and class conflicts (Geertz 1963), most of which have arisen from antagonism involving different ethnic or religious sentiments, values, and interests. These conflicts have posed a threat to the integrative existence of many Third World societies (Eisenstadt 1973; Smelser 1968), which has often been aggravated by their exploitation by major international powers and wealthy countries and their dependence on international markets (Amin 1977). Under such conditions many governments of developing societies have become regimented and are usually dominated by the military. While a regimented government may appear to unify a given society in the short run, it often lacks legitimacy and is too rigid to absorb all the divisive forces in the society.

Against the background of a strong potential for disintegration, due to acute primordial diversity and economic scarcity, the capacity of Indian society to function in a democratic manner and to institutionalize conflicts presents a "deviant" case among developing nations. Most countries with similar conditions have succumbed to a process of power struggles, total conflict, and social anomie, which has often resulted in civil war, governmental instability, or military rule. India, by contrast, has been relatively successful in maintaining political integration within a competitive framework. Taking this fact into account (in spite of the 1975 State of Emergency which was reversed by the March 1977 and January 1980 elections), it seems that India provides an excellent case for studying how conflicting patterns of legitimation and integration can coexist.

One school of thought predicts that India's diversity will ultimately lead to disintegration unless it shifts to an authoritarian regime (Harrison 1960; Moore 1966). Another insists that it has succeeded in countering centrifugal trends through the development of democratic institutions (Kothari 1970). Neither school, however, specifies the makeup of the socio-political institutions which would increase the probability that one form of regime evolves to the exclusion of the other. It is our thesis that Indian society has managed to sustain its unique democratic system by building institutions which accentuate the inherent conflicts, on the one hand, and yet mediate between antagonistic groups and sectors, on the other.

While the importance of intermediary groups that link diverse interests has long been recognized, the investigation of intermediary institutions has largely been neglected. Such institutions bridge the gap between different codes of behavior (and between groups committed to different rules), and institutionalize social conflict. Their special structures – entailing the coexistence of institutional and non- (or anti-) institutional arrangements – enable these institutions to function as bridging or mediatory mechanisms.

Mediatory mechanisms serve as arenas for negotiation in which the relationships among different primordial groups become more symmetrical. As a result of this process, the antagonistic groups mutually adjust their expectations and establish universal rules by which to institutionalize conflicts. India's ability to cope with conflicts through democratic means, despite its strong divisive elements, has been the result of such a process. It therefore makes a suitable case study for investigating the mechanisms by which legitimation and integration are sustained under conditions of conflict.

The economic situation in India, which has long been one of the country's most crucial problems, is used as a parameter throughout this monograph. The methodological validity of such an approach is based on the gradual nature of change in the Indian economy since the beginning of this century (Myrdal 1968). Several explanations have been suggested for this pace of economic change. Perhaps the more important ones point to the impact of colonial rule, economic scarcity and the growth in population, the nature of the caste structure and the enterpreneurial groups, and the Hindu religion. An alternative explanation is that the economy has been exploited for integrative purposes.

In examining the mechanisms that have enabled India to maintain a democratic regime in the face of strong divisiveness, this monograph takes into account not only criteria inherent to the Indian system but also general theoretical variables. The use of general theory enables us to place India (implicitly or explicitly) into a comparative context. The manuscript thus elaborates current sociological trends in four ways: (1) It goes beyond the common dichotomy of theories which view society as either a conflicting entity or an entity based on equilibrium, suggesting a model of society in which conflicts are accentuated for integrative purposes. (2) It illustrates the structure of the mechanisms by which antagonistic elements of society are connected. (3) It indicates the strategies through which common traditions are manipulated for new purposes. (4) It characterizes social order by the processes in which its different institutional spheres are fused rather than differentiated.

The monograph draws on primary and secondary sources of four types: (1) national statistics of authorized agents, such as the Central Bureau of Statistics; (2) historical and sociological studies; (3) documents of quasi-official British and Indian agents and institutionalized bodies or social movements; and (4) selected works and diaries of Indian and colonial public figures, leaders, and officials. We hope that the variety of sources has enabled us to somewhat balance the diverse interpretations of the Indian phenomenon.

The monograph is divided into nine chapters. We begin in Chapter One by presenting a theoretical framework for analyzing political legitimation and integration in transitional societies under conditions of high social diversity and antagonism. The second and third chapters, devoted to India's acute integration problems, concentrate on the most salient of the divisive factors that threaten the society's survival. Chapter Four discusses some central traditional patterns in India and their reconstruction into modern concepts of integration. Chapter Five deals with the formation and nature of the "carriers" of the modern concepts of integration, namely, the leaders of the Indian national movement and the educated elites. The sixth and seventh chapters, which explore the basic intermediary processes and bridging mechanisms by which India has maintained its democratic pattern, provide evidence indicating that despite the Western terminology applied to these mechanisms they often assume different structures and meanings in the Indian context. The eighth chapter deals with the boundaries of the Indian system and its intermediary mechanisms by analyzing the State of Emergency declared in June 1975 and the political shifts evinced in the 1977 and 1980 elections. The final chapter is an epilogue which discusses the meaning of recent events in India in the light of our conceptual framework.

While we do not pretend to have done justice to the entire subject, we have endeavored to show the internal logic of the Indian case and to utilize it to extend some sociological perspectives.

The research is part of a broader program under the auspices of the Comparative Civilizations and Modernization Unit at the Harry S. Truman Research Institute for the Advancement of Peace of the Hebrew University of Jerusalem.

I would like to thank the Institute for International Studies at the University of California, Berkeley, and the Harry S. Truman Research Institute for providing the funds for my visits to India. I am also grateful to the Center of South Asian Studies at the University of Cambridge for their hospitality. During the preparation of this monograph, I benefited greatly from the comments of many people, among them Professor N.J. Smelser, the late Professor I. Vallier, and Professors S.N. Eisenstadt, H.Z. Schiffrin, M.S.A. Rao, B. Narain, M. Brecher, M. Weiner, and W.H. Morris-Jones. I was also fortunate to enjoy the editorship and comments of Mrs. H. Hogri, Mrs. R. Anug, Mrs. S. Azulay, and Mrs. B. Misrachi, and to have had Miss N. Schneider, Director of Publications of the Truman Institute, oversee the editing and production of the manuscript.

Chapter 1

THEORETICAL FRAMEWORK

INTRODUCTION

Major social change involves the transformation of the basic value premises, the institutional arrangements, and the position of most groups in a given society. In that sense, social change may be said to have the potential to cause the bases of social legitimation and integration to erode.

The concept of "legitimation" is defined as a set of value-oriented premises considered fair by large parts of a given society and used by that society to justify the specific patterns of the social order. In functional terms, the greater the legitimacy of a social order, the greater the probability that certain rules and patterns of behavior will be institutionalized. The concept of "integration" may be broadly defined as the interdependence of different (and sometimes conflicting) social elements, including rules, interest groups, and institutional sectors. Assuming that every social system incorporates antagonistic ingredients to some degree, conditions of social change may accentuate this antagonism to the point where the probability of maintaining integration is extremely low. The central question, therefore, is how antagonism can be absorbed into the system without paralyzing it.

On the more operative level, both legitimation and integration can be said to refer to the dynamic processes and mechanisms by which different and even antagonistic elements are bridged. In that sense, legitimation is utilized here as a symbolic device by which different values or norms are linked, while integration refers to the processes by which social conflicts are institutionalized.

The aim of this chapter is to explain theoretically how societies cope with structural antagonism — that is, antagonism embodied into their very framework — under transitional conditions. In the chapters that follow we shall validate this construct by relating it to the case of India.

The chapter is divided into three main sections. In the first, the scope of antagonistic elements and the way they cluster will be briefly presented to reveal the acuteness of the problem in terms of legitimation and integration. The second section will briefly explore major theoretical approaches toward its solution. Finally, we shall expand upon the theories of legitimation and integration to explain how structural antagonism is institutionalized.

1

BASES OF STRUCTURAL ANTAGONISM

Most developing societies comprise several autonomous primordial groups (be they religious, tribal, linguistic, or racial) that maintain few common symbols and norms, and whose level of interdependence is low. During the process of change primordial differences tend to be accentuated, often being transformed into violent clashes (Emerson, 1960; Geertz, 1963). Change also accentuates problems of economic scarcity. When the population increases without a parallel increase in productivity, the struggle for shares in the national pie is enhanced (Myrdal, 1969). Rising aspirations, together with the unequal distribution of national wealth, increase the sense of deprivation and injustice (Scott, 1976). Under such conditions class differences are also accentuated, and class struggle, partially congruent with primordial differences, is very likely to develop. The antagonism is exacerbated because most developing societies are multiple in structure, i.e., are divided horizontally into different sectors dominated by contradictory principles (Boeke, 1953; Hoselitz, 1966; Nash, 1964). In addition, multiplicity is often accompanied by structural divergence.

The concept "divergence"[1] will be used here to indicate a process whereby two or more institutions develop in different directions and to varying degrees. If occupational opportunities do not expand at the same rate as educational possibilities, the two spheres can be said to diverge. The same is true when economic institutions are modernized and political institutions remain "traditional," or vice versa. When slow economic growth is accompanied by rapid development of open and competitive political institutions, the opportunities for aggregating power exceed those for accumulating wealth, and the former can easily become inflated. This tendency is expressed in the spread of small political factors largely based on local primordial ties, each faction attempting to convert its political power into material goods. Where this situation is accompanied by economic scarcity, the power struggle is accentuated and the potential for disintegration rises.

Another aspect of divergence — namely, the cultural and institutional gap between ruling center and periphery found in most developing societies (Shils, 1975; Weiner, 1975) — often poses a threat to social integration, particularly when it is aggravated by rising expectations. Most established elites are then faced with a dilemma. If they enlarge economic and political participation to increase support, their privileges will be reduced. However, if they exploit their position to reduce peripheral benefits and participation, their legitimacy will be endangered. Most new elites in developing countries choose the second alternative even though such a strategy may eventually cause frustration to accumulate in the periphery. This brings about the erosion of legitimacy, thereby increasing the probability of disintegration. However, the rapid transfer to full engagement of peripheral groups may have similar results.

To conclude, transitional societies are faced with the irresolvable problem of legitimizing a social system composed of antagonistic values, while attempting to keep conflicting forces within an operative framework, a problem that has been dealt with by sociologists over the past half century. The following brief review of relevant theoretical approaches will be discussed from one perspective only: the extent to which they contribute to an understanding of how an antagonistic social structure can function.

THEORETICAL SOLUTIONS TO THE PROBLEMS OF LEGITIMACY AND INTEGRATION

Issues of legitimation and integration have often been perceived and treated as one problem. For the sake of clarity we will attempt to analyze them separately, keeping in mind that there is a great deal of overlap between the two.

Theories of Legitimation

The problem of antagonistic patterns of legitimacy has been approached from a number of directions. Each of the four approaches discussed below suggests a different solution.

Tocqueville concerned himself with changes in the principles of legitimacy and with the development of marginal situations of commitment in countries that shifted from aristocratic monarchies to democratic republics: "...epochs sometimes occur in the life of a nation when the old customs of a people are changed, public morality is destroyed, religious belief shaken, and the spell of tradition broken...." The citizens then have "neither the instinctive patriotism of a monarchy nor the reflecting patriotism of a republic.... They have stopped between the two in a midst of confusion and distress" (Tocqueville, 1961: I, 251–252). While Tocqueville did not explain how a stable regime can be legitimized under such conditions, his implicit solution to the problem of antagonistic patterns of legitimacy is clear: antagonism can be utilized only when differences are institutionalized within a social framework in which every component is tolerated (i.e., a pluralistic society) (Tocqueville, 1961: II, 99ff).

Max Weber suggested that empirical modified versions of so-called "ideal types" of legitimacy can function together within the same framework (1947:30). In his well-known distinction between traditional, charismatic, and legal-rational sources of legitimacy, he indirectly hinted at three ways in which these patterns may be interchanged: they may be differentiated, combined (e.g., institutionalized charisma), or connected through a "constellation of interests" and compromise (Weber, 1954:324).

Ferrero perceived legitimacy as a dynamic process containing four consecutive stages: pre-legitimacy, quasi-legitimacy, legitimacy, and illegitimacy. At the stage of quasi-legitimacy there is no single source of legitimacy but rather a clash between conflicting principles (Ferrero, 1942:217). Ferrero did not, however, specify how the transition can be made from quasi-legitimacy to legitimacy.

Finally, Selznick discussed the concept of legitimation in terms of the link between concrete interests and general principles:

> Legitimation can begin in a quite primitive fashion. It may mean little more than unconscious acceptance of someone's authority because he is thought to have communication with the gods, or special magical powers, or because he belongs to a noble family.... There need not be any awareness of the habit of thought involved, nor surely any self-consciousness regarding the abstract connection between exercised authority and an underlying principle of legitimacy.... A primitive legitimacy speaks only to the *gross* justification of a claim to hold office. The relevant writ is *quo warranto*, which runs against the usurper.... Legality is extended in *depth*, used to query *particular* acts and policies (Selznick, 1969:30).

The uniqueness of Selznick's approach lies in his pointing out that legitimacy cannot be identified solely with legal authority but must be based on concepts of justice anchored in universal values. Furthermore, universal values must be translated into particularistic interests. It is through this combination that a social order is legitimized. What is not clear, however, is how particularistic and universalistic elements can be combined without paralyzing the whole social structure.

From an analytical standpoint, what is common to these four approaches is that they recognize the inherent antagonism in principles of legitimacy and suggest different frameworks in which to combine them. They do not, however, demonstrate the nature of such a combination or the devices by which it operates. Bearing this theoretical framework in mind, let us now move on to theories regarding the problem of integration.

Theories of Integration

Analytically, one may distinguish six major approaches to integration. The first defines integration or solidarity as being based on a division of labor and therefore on different kinds of functional, horizontal patterns of interdependence (Durkheim, 1964). The second is the theory of dependency, a modern version of the Marxist approach, according to which integration follows a vertical pattern in which a powerful party exploits and controls weak groups or countries (Frank, 1967, Hechter, 1975). A third approach views integration as a statistical average of the strengths of different groups, based on the amount and kind of resources (power, wealth, prestige) they hold (Eisenstadt, 1965). The fourth, a pluralistic approach, measures integration according to the degree of overlapping group membership. It is assumed that the larger the overlap, the greater the solidarity (Kuper, 1971). A fifth approach defines integration in terms of the number and severity of conflicts among different social sectors (Dahrendorf, 1959). The last approach referred to here considers the kind and amount of institutional mechanisms used to cope with potential frustration and conflicts (Apter, 1961; Eisenstadt, 1965, 1973; Smelser, 1968).

It is this last approach that will serve as our point of departure. We shall expand upon it and the other theories by viewing antagonism as a source of change rather than of instability, by shifting attention from the intensity of conflicts to the degree and pattern in which they are absorbed into the system, and by investigating the mechanisms which enable the absorption and operation of such conflicts.

TOWARD A THEORY OF INTERMEDIARY INSTITUTIONS

To understand how it is possible to operate antagonistic patterns of legitimation and integration, it is necessary to specify the mechanisms by which antagonistic elements are combined and utilized, and the conditions under which these mechanisms emerge. One may distinguish five patterns in which contradictory principles can be connected: differentiated, mixed, reconciled, brokerage, and fused.

In the differentiated pattern each principle and arrangement is utilized in different situations, roles, and institutional contexts, and they are also functionally interlinked; while this largely helps to avoid conflicts, it may, at the same time, reinforce antagonisms. In the mixed pattern contradictory principles are blended and used simultaneously in any given situation or institutional context; this facilitates the development of social anomie. In the reconciled type antagonism is mitigated by maintaining a low profile for each principle; social change may consequently be slowed down.

In the brokerage pattern different codes and elements of society are connected but not fused. Brokerage mechanisms contribute to social exchange among different groups, but keep them socially distinct. For example, a middleman is supplied with raw materials, which he sells to customers in the market; he then uses the money earned to buy goods with which he pays his suppliers. Therefore, while customers and suppliers are connected, they are not involved with each other.

In fusion, perhaps the only pattern in which contradictions can be used to legitimize and integrate transitional societies, contradictions are combined into a single entity with the aid of intermediary bridging mechanisms[2] which translate and implement concepts and rules, thereby directly linking divergent principles and parts of society. The basic components of intermediary mechanisms are: (1) exhaustiveness: they include most aspects of a given life situation with minimal differentiation between them; (2) structural complexity: they contain many different codes of behavior; (3) institutional ambiguousness: relationships between the codes are loosely defined; (4) open structure:

they are structured to provide an arena for bargaining among particularistic powers; and (5) symmetry: they involve an exchange between relatively equal or equivalent parties which mutually adjust their expectations and interests.

The components of intermediary mechanisms are linked as follows. Exhaustiveness assures that all contradictory forces are kept under one roof, thereby leading to structural complexity. Structural complexity allows for the operation of an ambiguous framework where the boundaries for negotiation are extended. Open boundaries weaken the traditional hierarchy as well as class differences, allowing the bargaining which takes place to be conducted between relatively equal parties. Relative equality means that no one group can force another to accept its terms; rather, groups must mutually accommodate to and use generalized rules of exchange based on the principle of reciprocity. Under such conditions, values and rules are considered fair, and their chances of being universalistic and thus institutionalized increase. General rules of behavior are most likely to be established when symmetry prevails because it provides a common setting for interaction between particularistic forces, thereby transforming conflicts into integrative devices.

Mediatory mechanisms should operate on both symbolic and organizational levels, symbolic mechanisms mediating between different values and norms, and organizational mechanisms connecting different groups and social institutions. Symbolic mechanisms alone may have little effect on concrete implementation, while the sole use of organizational mechanisms places legitimacy in doubt. Thus, full mediatory power depends on how the two levels are combined. In addition, the distribution of mechanisms over various institutional spheres (e.g., political, legal, educational) increases their intermediary power, because it provides alternative channels to cope with potential conflict.

The conditions under which mediatory mechanisms are formed and articulated are beyond the scope of this monograph. However, a few general comments seem warranted.

Mediatory mechanisms seem to emerge and operate under three related conditions: (1) when the basis of division between particularistic forces and antagonistic principles is universally defined (since such a definition provides a common basis for negotiation); (2) when "mechanical" (primordial) and "organic" (functional) patterns of division of labor overlap and clash in a dialectical way,[3] that is, when primordial affiliations are sporadically utilized as bases for class organization, and class organization, for primordial affiliations; and (3) when a special kind of dual actor is available — an agent who dominates the resources relevant to competing (e.g., established and emerging) cultures, and who can therefore interpret and manipulate them. Under conditions of transition and structural multiplicity, such actors are marginal individuals or groups, anchored in two or more types of values, and controlling different kinds of resources.[4] Their role can be defined as the "dynamic organization of norms and counter-norms" (Merton and Barber, 1963:103). The emergence of such actors seems to depend on the nature of traditional elites, their position in society, and above all on the patterns and channels through which they emerge.[5] It can also be assumed that the elites will be interested in perpetuating their dominant and privileged positions, and will use the least expensive devices available to accomplish this. Perhaps the most efficient way for elites to enhance their position under transitional conditions is to utilize mediatory mechanisms, which assure them maximal usage of old values and new arrangements, the new arrangements providing the setting for a special pattern of legitimacy and integration in which particularistic units are organized competitively.

Cooperation among groups is made possible by the formation of short-term ad hoc coalitions which vary according to the particular issue at stake. The social structure in which this takes place is based on shifting foci of antagonism, with the mediatory institutions providing an arena for managing, channelling and institutionalizing clashes.

Against its background of high diversity and major conflicts, the capacity of Indian society to establish a relatively stable democratic regime makes India an adequate case for applying the above theoretical approach.

NOTES

1. For the definition of the concept of divergence, see Baum, 1974; Eisenstadt, 1973; Meyer et al., 1975.

2. For the importance of intermediary groups and institutions as integrating factors, see Burke, 1955; Durkheim, 1964; Geertz, 1963; Shils, 1975; Tocqueville, 1961.

3. The concept of dialectics is used here in two senses. Firstly, it denotes a three-phase pattern consisting of an initial stage, a counterstage, and a synthesis of the two that does not, however, eliminate the conflicts. Secondly, it is used as a methodological device referring to a certain type of logic in which elements are inconsistent, diverse, or even contradictory. This logic not only serves as a phenomenological device but can also be used to describe empirical processes.

The above definitions have been borrowed from Hegel's logic as it appeared in the *Encyclopaedia of Philosophical Sciences* in 1830. Hegel defined dialectics in a number of ways. For example, he claimed that the term "meant the indwelling tendency outwards by which the one-sidedness and limitation of the predicates of understanding is seen in its true light and shown to be the negation of them" (1975:1169, S81). Hegel also assumed that the "world can best be explained as composed of antinomies"; that is, "it maintains two opposite propositions about the same object... in such a way that each of them has to be maintained with equal necessity" (1975:76, S48). He further assumed that antinomies "appear in all objects of every kind, in all conceptions, notions, ideas and spheres of life" (1975:76, S48). Thus, for example, "in political life... extreme anarchy and extreme despotism naturally lead to one another" (1975:118, S81).

4. Significant actors familiar with two or more cultural codes can operate between two spheres (as marginal men), within two spheres (as middlemen), in fused spheres (as hybrid types), or within differentiated spheres. In all of these manifestations, however, they act as a link between two or more distinct cultures and institutional frameworks. For the definition of the marginal man, see Gist and Wright, 1973; R.E. Park, 1928; Press, 1969; Stonequist, 1964:341. The middleman is defined by Hanna and Hanna, 1967:21; the hybrid or fused type is partially described by Stonequist, 1964:341; and the differentiated type is discussed by Pye, 1958:345.

5. For an analysis of the background which fosters significant actors, see Kahane, 1975.

Chapter 2

PRIMORDIAL BARRIERS TO INTEGRATION

INTRODUCTION

There are two largely opposing views regarding the survivability of the Indian pattern of democracy. The first sees India as composed of such diversities and antagonism that it cannot remain an integrated society in the long run without adopting a regimented, authoritarian pattern of regime (Harrison, 1960; Moore, 1966). In contrast, the second claims that India has been able to counter its centrifugal trends by modernizing its tradition and developing flexible institutions (Kothari, 1970a; Rudolph and Rudolph, 1967; Weiner, 1967).

The existence of such opposing views demands an analysis of the basic diversities and antagonism inherent in Indian society. Such an analysis is also a necessary tool for understanding the logic behind one of the major processes with which this monograph is concerned: the utilization of conflicting forces to legitimize acceptable rules for integrating Indian society. While this subject has been widely discussed in the literature, we feel a description of impediments to Indian integration is justified in light of its relevance to our later discussion of the ways in which Indian society has coped with the problem of its social system.

Generally speaking, primordial divisions tend to be intensified under conditions of rapid social change and nation-building (Geertz, 1963). More specifically, the attempt to unify different groups through the universal, egalitarian concept of nationhood tends to accentuate primordial division. A split along these lines is generally an indication of weak "non-contractual" elements and basic distrust, which may endanger the very basis of legitimation and integration in a society. Class, economic, and political differences often overlap and reinforce primordial splits, thereby adding a functional flavor and reducing the potential for societal integration.

Most splits and disputes in developing societies are "total" in three senses: they encompass both symbolic and institutional aspects of society, primordial and non-primordial factors, as well as all spheres of life.

In India, as in other developing societies, primordial and class (non-primordial) factors often overlap and reinforce one another (Bhatt, 1975). The relative weight of each primordial and non-primordial factor and the way in which they interlink vary from region to region and from one societal level to another. Primordial factors are sometimes activated as unifying cross-class elements (V. Singh, 1973); other times class factors link different primordial groups. Thus, our concern here with primordial elements refers not only to the existing splits, but also to the process by which these factors determine occupational, economic, political, and educational expectations and opportunities.

We open our discussion of the potential for disintegration in India with a brief review of the major primordial divisions. We shall continue with a description of non-primordial splits in the following chapter. Structural dualism and divergence will be discussed in both contexts. Our analysis of economic conditions, as well as the sources of deprivation and discontent in the Indian system, will also cross-cut the two subjects.

PRIMORDIAL SPLITS: LANGUAGE, RELIGION, CASTE

Although in modern Western societies primordial associations have recently been utilized by minorities to promote their occupational, political, and educational interests, they are nevertheless often considered a socially pathological phenomenon. In India, on the other hand, the most common pattern since at least the beginning of the century has been the utilization of primordial associations. The most salient primordial factors which will be discussed here are language, religion, and caste.

Language

Language can be conceived first as a necessary (but insufficient) tool for communication among different groups. It may also be an important determinant of cultural identity (Cassirer, 1955). More pragmatically, language can be perceived as an instrument which determines a differentiated pattern of access to economic and political positions (Fishman et al., 1968). It is a primordial phenomenon in both the collective and the individual sense since it is accumulated through generations and transmitted almost unconsciously in the early stages of socialization. In that respect, it symbolically becomes a "typifying schemata" (Schutz and Luckmann, 1974). Consequently, its impact may extend over both cultural and instrumental aspects of life. Further, it often appears as a labeling factor which further reinforces cultural and economic splits.

Language division in India is perhaps one of the country's most central problems and has long been studied (J. Das Gupta, 1970; Prakash, 1973; G.N. Srivastava, 1970; Yadav, 1969). Here we shall not be concerned with the history of the problem or with all its aspects and ramifications. Our main point is that, despite (or because of) official policy, language division is still an important divisive factor. What is equally important is the tendency of some linguistic groups to crystallize in political terms (J. Das Gupta, 1970: Ch. IV). In this connection, language rivalry has often been the basis of class and political associations (J. Das Gupta, 1970: Ch.V). The attempts to impose linguistic homogeneity in India (Hindi, English, or other vernacular languages) have accentuated the problem. Any attempt to rely on particular languages deprives those groups who are unable to use it and reduces their chances of gaining access to occupational positions, government posts, and educational institutions.

The 1971 census classified the Indian languages into four families. The most important of these in terms of number of speakers are the Indo-European family (321 million) and the Dravidian (107 million) (Nigam, 1971). Table 2:1 indicates the twenty most important languages in India and the number of people who speak them.

The language division potentially splits India into various sections which can hardly communicate with one another. Harrison (1960) and J. Das Gupta (1970) have both pointed out the strong emotional appeal of linguistic separatism which has often been transformed into political power emphasizing strong particularistic interests. Any attempt at unification in linguistic terms means a significant increase in the local sense of deprivation and may endanger the solidarity of the Indian Union if it includes a large enough section of the population. On the other hand, the continuation of language division means the perpetuation of Indian splits as well as the inferior position of various linguistic minorities.

The significance of language division as a disintegrative factor lies not only in the absence of a common national language and lack of opportunities for wider communication among different groups, but also in the impingement of regional and state affiliations on linguistic identities. The congruence of language and region provides a basic denominator of particularistic identity, threatening Indian integration. Language differences sometimes embody communal sentiments as well as cultural and religious distinctions, although the intensity of feelings varies in different regions (Bondurant, 1958:49; J. Das Gupta, 1970; *Seminar*, March 1969:115). For example, the dispute between the Tamils in the south and the governing center in the north is basically a regional conflict based on linguistic and racial differences (Dravidians vs. Aryans) which has been transformed into clear-cut political antagonism (Dravida Munnetra Kazhagam [DMK] vs. Congress Party).[1] With reference to the Muslim minority, the Urdu language is sometimes highly correlated with religious sentiments (J. Das Gupta, 1970:123), often imparting a religious flavor to the linguistic split.

Religion

Religion is another primordial factor which largely determines individual and collective identity, values, and group loyalties and is therefore considered

TABLE 2:1

POPULATION DISTRIBUTION BY FIRST LANGUAGE
(Provisional Figures from the 1967 Census)

Language Community	Population	Percentage of Total Population
Hindi	153,729,062	28.1
Telugu	44,707,697	8.2
Bengali	44,521,533	8.1
Marathi	41,723,893	7.6
Tamil	37,592,794	6.9
Urdu	28,600,428	5.2
Gujarati	25,656,274	4.7
Malayalam	21,917,430	4.0
Kannada	21,575,019	3.9
Oriya	19,726,745	3.6
Bhojpuri	14,340,564	2.6
Punjabi	13,900,202	2.5
Assamese	8,958,977	1.6
Chhattisgarhi	6,693,445	1.2
Magahi/Magadhi	6,638,495	1.2
Maithili	6,121,922	1.1
Marwari	4,714,094	0.9
Santali	3,693,558	0.7
Kashmiri	2,421,760	0.4
Rajasthani	2,093,557	0.4
Others	38,622,360	7.1
Total Population	547,949,809	100.0

Source: Computed from R.C. Nigam, *Language Handbook on Mother Tongues in Census,* Census Centenary Monograph No. 10, New Delhi: Office of the Registrar General, Ministry of Home Affairs, p. 333.

an important divisive factor in India. Religion is defined here as a dynamic set of more or less absolute codes, anchored in transcendental premises which fully or partially determine various patterns of faith and behavior. What is important is that religion has individual and collective significance as well as cognitive and sentimental meaning.

Religious belief and organization can easily be converted into an instrument by which interests can be manipulated. Conflicts based on language diversification are not necessarily value-oriented, but those based on religious differences may denote a lack of consensus on basic social premises. In addition, value-oriented conflicts are usually charged with strong emotions.

Both value commitments and sentiments determine strong moral boundaries between groups and can easily be transformed into violent conflicts. When religious differences impinge, to some extent, on socio-economic differences, they receive an instrumental flavor and their power is reinforced.

Indian society is composed of a majority of various Hindu groups, a large Muslim minority, and a number of smaller minorities (see Table 2:2). The most important religious division is obviously between Hindu and Muslim groups. Traditionally, the religious codes of Islam are quite different from those of Hinduism, such that the Muslim community has never been fully absorbed into the Hindu community or its institutional structure, and it has not been capable of accommodating to it (Dalwai, 1968; Hardy, 1972; Lal, 1973; Lokhandwalla, 1971; Robinson, 1974; Sharif, 1972).

TABLE 2:2

POPULATION DISTRIBUTION BY MAIN RELIGIONS
(1971)

Major Religious Communities	Population	Percentage of Total Population
Hindu	453,292,086	82.72
Muslims	61,417,934	11.21
Christians	14,223,382	2.60
Sikhs	10,378,797	1.89
Buddhists	3,812,325	0.70
Jains	2,604,646	0.47

Source: Religion, in *Census of India 1971,* Series 1, "India," p. iii.

The situation is further complicated by a few additional factors. The collective memory of Muslim dominancy in India has made their accommodation (as a community) psychologically difficult. The size of their community and their demographic qualities have accentuated the problem (Lal, 1973). As the largest minority they have been able to organize separate communal institutions, such as the Muslim League, and therefore pose a threat to the Hindu majority (Panikkar, 1963:60). In addition, the existence of parallel Muslim institutions alongside national ones has limited the possibilities of developing conflict-solving mechanisms.

An important historical example of the high level of conflict based on religious divisions is the outbreak in Kerala which erupted between Hindus and Muslims prior to partition (1921/22), what has been termed the Mappila Rebellion. The outbreak has been explained largely as a result of class conflict between Muslim merchants and Hindu landlords (Dale, 1978; Dhanagare, 1977; Hardgrave, 1977; R.E. Miller, 1976). Actually, the conflict was charged with religious sentiments that eventually became more important than class factors. Furthermore, the conflict was also connected to the caste structure: the fact that some Hindu lower castes had undergone conversion to Islam was considered a threat by Hindu upper castes (Dale, 1978). From our point of view, the severity of the clash between Muslims and Hindus was determined by their limited ability to cope with conflict through institutional means owing to the existence of the parallel communities.

The consolidation of the Indian national movement at the beginning of the twentieth century accentuated tensions between the two communities and reinforced the parallel institutions. In the pre-partition period, the Muslims' strongest argument against full integration into Indian society was based on the assumption that, due to its ascriptive exclusiveness, the Hindu caste structure could not coexist with democracy (Latif, 1939:5). They were afraid that the communal particularistic forces of the majority would be utilized to destroy and transform them into a helpless minority. Thus, the partition of India into different cultural and political zones was perceived as the only solution (Latif, 1939:4–5).

Muslim suspicions were reinforced by the fact that Indian nationalism was based, to some extent, on elements of Hindu tradition. Although Gandhi attempted to give a universal, secular flavor to these elements, Muslims still considered them to be purely Hindu ideas (Ali, 1967; Latif, 1939:15). Hindus themselves were in a dilemma in this respect: to mobilize the support of the masses they had to utilize some traditional Hindu elements, which eventually reduced the chances of integrating the Muslim minority.

From the viewpoints of Muslims and Hindus alike, the partition of India in 1947 was an act of integration or at least an institutional recognition of the existence of parallel communities. The partition was not only along religious lines but also along non-primordial ones. Misra (1976) described the partition as the result of a clash between the Hindu upper-middle class (which dominates the Congress Party) and the Muslim counter-political elite.

The partition of India and the establishment of Pakistan reduced the Muslim minority from approximately twenty-five percent in British India to about ten percent of the total population in post-partition India. From the Hindu point of view, this made the religious problem less acute. Conversely, the situation became more problematic from the Muslim point of view. To facilitate the integration of the Muslims, the Indian Union was created as a secular state. The official differentiation between state and religion was expected to reduce religious tension (Galanter, 1971; V.K. Sinha, 1969; D.E. Smith, 1963). The result, however, has often been perceived as an attempt to leave the religious minorities to the mercy of the civic institutions, most of which are dominated by the Hindu majority (Gauba, 1973).

Although the institutionalization of Muslim political representation and that of other minorities in various positions in the government and in the political parties has somewhat mitigated the problem, many scholars have recognized that, as long as the religious elements are not differentiated from the political ones, full integration of the society, at least regarding the Muslim minority, is doubtful (Dalwai, 1968; Panikkar, 1963). Furthermore, due to the basic differences between Muslim and Hindu beliefs and institutions, the creation of various mechanisms to cope with conflict is also very difficult.[2] In fact, some parts of the Muslim and Hindu communities have established separate collective identities and often regard one another as enemies. Such distinct definitions open the way for a community professing one religion to attack a different religious community without referring to any non-contractual elements or institutional boundaries.[3]

Religious divisions are also frequently manipulated for political and economic purposes. For example, Gould (1966:51–52) notes that the Jan Sangh Party in Uttar Pradesh used religious symbols to gain power and mobilize commitment. Politicians have usually utilized divisions to promote their interests, thereby having a negative impact on national integration (Kothari, 1970a, 1970b). Mobilization of political support through religious groups is efficient and relatively cheap. Thus, even secular parties are often forced to utilize religious sentiments to mobilize support. Under these conditions, religious factors are often converted into prejudices and stereotypes. This adds a psychological-irrational dimension to the religious clashes (Ghouse, 1973:83).

What is equally important is that religious sentiments often tend to crystallize into extreme militant associations. The emergence of such associations among the Hindus can be exemplified by the Anand Marg, which claims 100,000 supporters, and the Rashtriya Swayam Sevak Sangh (RSS), which is related to the Jan Sangh (Ghouse, 1973:65). The rise of such groups may point to an ongoing process of polarization along religious lines and may indicate the explosive nature of the religious division.

Aside from the major clashes between Muslims and Hindus, other religious divisions in India have also resulted in conflict, as exemplified by the dispute between Sikhs and Hindus in Punjab. In November 1966, following a number of clashes, Punjab was split into two states: a predominantly Hindu Haryana state and a Sikh-dominated Punjab state. Each community demanded exclusive possession of the capital city. Prime Minister Indira Gandhi promised to resolve the dispute once the 1967 elections were over. In the meantime, Chandigarh remained the capital of both states. In January 1970 Mrs. Gandhi decided that the Sikhs should have the capital and the Hindus should receive compensation in the form of $26 million for a new capital. The reaction to this solution was a recurrence of violent riots.

A brief analysis of the structure of religious communal clashes (sometimes combined with class-oriented interests) may help explain how easily these conflicts can be transformed into a societal breakdown. Essentially, communal clashes can be analyzed within the general "value added" model (Smelser, 1962, 1968). However, there are a few unique features in this model regarding the Indian case. As has been illustrated, "objective" conditions conducive to clashes (e.g., primordial divisions as well as the existing sense of anxiety and deprivation) have been common to India. Most riots are initiated by a minor event which catalyzes the "objective" potential and transforms it into an actual conflict. Small incidents are usually reinforced by the spread of rumors, which add a strong sentimental element. Equally important, each outbreak has a cultural symbolic dimension combined with real interests. In addition, each of the disputing parties is backed by an organization capable of managing the conflict. Some of the riots occur in the context of an institutional vacuum, that is, in a transitional situation where neither "old" nor "new" institutions are capable of intervening in the various stages of the dispute or where their involvement actually reinforces the clash. Under the above conditions not only are religious conflicts accentuated, but also the institutions meant to cope with the problem generally tend to be weakened or identified as biased or communal.

Religious splits, especially those between Hindus and Muslims, have exposed one of the major dilemmas of Indian legitimation and integration. On the one hand, denying religious symbols may make the whole concept of nationhood meaningless; on the other, the utilization of religious symbols necessarily alienates the non-Hindu communities, thereby splitting the nation. Thus, religion as a divisive factor is culturally and structurally immanent to Indian society.

Caste

The Hindu majority can hardly be considered a homogeneous and unified group. Divisions in the Hindu communities are based on differences on both the pragmatical and transcendental levels of religion (Mandelbaum, 1964:10, 1970; Srinivas, 1969) and are reflected on both local and national levels.

There are different definitions of the concept of caste (i.e., *jati, varna*). Perhaps the two polar conceptions of caste can be defined as fluctuating between those who see it as a symbolic, prestige-oriented, or cult-oriented unit, stressing its ritualistic aspects (i.e., purity and impurity) (Dumont, 1970: 36–39) and those who conceive caste more as a socio-economic unit or almost a class (Bailey, 1963; Berreman, 1965). In fact, many possible caste classifications exist, the most important of which are occupation, prestige, and wealth (Madan, 1971).

There is no one-to-one relationship between caste and class, wealth and prestige, wealth and religious ritualistic positions, or caste and religious position. For our purposes, the most important aspect of caste (*jati*) is its diffuse primordial character. It is a social unit which includes all aspects of life in an undifferentiated way from both social and individual standpoints. Following Fox (1969a), it is suggested that a *jati* is a group based on locality, kinship, delimitation, endogamy, hypergamy, commensalism, occupational specialization, and juridical corporate functions.

Caste divisions clearly represent the most basic split in India. The traditional four *varnas* of Hinduism are subdivided into more than 3,000 *jatis* based on ascriptive affiliations on the local level (Hutton, 1963; Mandelbaum, 1970). Ideally speaking, the *jati* division in traditional India was a stable integrative system, based on exclusive groupings with definite rank, order, and functions. These differentiations integrated the country in a semi-"organic" type of solidarity (see our discussion in Ch.4). The introduction of competitive principles into the caste system by the British (or earlier) increased its disintegrative potential (Bailey, 1960, 1963; Berreman, 1965; Madan, 1971; Srinivas, 1969).

Once a quasi-open political and economic system had been set up, the *jati* system became a potential source of conflict on the local and national levels. Once *jatis* competed with one another by using their traditional commitments and loyalties in open election markets, a "war of all against all" could ensue. As various scholars have shown (Brass, 1974; J.M. Brown, 1972:328; Irschick, 1969; Saraswathi, 1974), the occurrence of sporadic clashes between local *jatis* became intensified from the second decade of the twentieth century, when British political reforms were extended and the articulation of national sentiment was increased. The primordial differences among castes were reinforced by the fact that they often represented different class interests and political organizations (Rudolph and Rudolph, 1967). The tension was further accentuated by the conversion of the "objective" differences into "subjective" attitudes and prejudices.

In sum, primordial divisions in India touch upon the very core of personal and collective identities so that differences are diffused and almost constant (Ghurye, 1969: Ch.14). Further divisions in terms of language, religion, and caste are accentuated when combined with socio-economic interests and other non-primordial elements.

NOTES

    1. The Tamil case and the Dravidian political organizations (the DMK) have been discussed by Hardgrave, 1969; Irschick, 1969; Jagannathan, 1968; Ram, 1968. See also the 1956 report of the Official Language Commission and the reports of the Commissioner for Linguistic Minorities.

    2. For further analysis of the problem, see Friedmann, 1976; "The Indian Muslims, A Symposium on the Attitudes of a Major Minority," *Seminar* 174, February, 1974.

    3. A detailed description of intra-religious clashes can be found almost daily in Indian newspapers. What is significant is the way they are interpreted by different primordial groups. See, for example, Madhok, 1970.

Chapter 3

NON-PRIMORDIAL BARRIERS TO INTEGRATION

INTRODUCTION

Non-primordial elements are usually considered more fluid than primordial factors because they are formed and based on flexible economic characteristics. This generalization, however, is not entirely applicable in the Indian context. Limited economic change, with regard to the level and distribution of per capita income and opportunities for mobility, has made class and political affiliations in India somewhat stagnant. This stagnancy, when accompanied by a rise in expectations among the lower classes, has accentuated splits and reinforced barriers for integration.

This chapter will analyze these divisive elements in relation to the caste, religious, and language divisions described in Chapter 2, and will show how primordial and non-primordial elements substitute for and/or complement each other.

THE ECONOMIC CONTEXT: SCARCITY AND DEPRIVATION

India is one of the poorest countries in the world in both relative (comparison of past and present per capita income) and absolute terms (Mukherjee and Chatterjee, 1974:252). Before reviewing the statistics, it should be noted that official economic objectives in the early fifties were "to raise the standard of living of the people and to open out to them opportunities for a richer and more varied life" (*The First Five Year Plan*, 1952:1). By the late seventies, official policy had come to declare that "it is a cause of legitimate national pride that over this period a stagnant and dependent economy has been modernized and made more self-reliant. A modest rate of growth of per capita income has been maintained despite the growth of population" (*Draft Five Year Plan, 1978–1983*, p. 1). Despite this modest rise in net national product (see Table 3:1) and per capita income, India's conditions of scarcity have only slightly improved, as may be inferred by the overall statistical evidence.

The Indian national income grew from $3.5 billion in 1931/32 to $32.4 billion in 1962/63, but about two thirds of this growth was negated by population expansion. There was an estimated decline in output per capita between

TABLE 3:1

ESTIMATES OF NATIONAL PRODUCT
FOR THE PERIOD 1950/1951 to 1973/1974

| | Net National Product | | | | Percentage Increase over Previous Year (at 1960/1961 Prices) | |
| | At Current Prices | | At 1960/1961 Prices | | | |
	Total (Rs crores)	Per Capita (Rs)	Total (Rs crores)	Per Capita (Rs)	Total	Per Capita
1950/51	8699	242.3	9078	252.9	–	–
1951/52	9037	254.2	9279	254.2	2.21	0.51
1952/53	8825	237.2	9590	257.8	3.35	1.42
1953/54	9480	250.1	10201	269.2	6.37	4.42
1954/55	8606	223.0	10483	271.6	2.76	0.89
1955/56	9123	232.1	10860	276.3	3.60	1.73
1956/57	10543	262.9	11461	285.8	5.53	3.44
1957/58	10540	257.7	11254	275.2	(–) 1.81	(–) 3.71
1958/59	11826	282.9	12165	291.0	8.09	5.74
1959/60	12211	286.6	12399	291.1	1.92	0.03
1960/61	13267	305.7	13267	305.7	7.00	5.02
1961/62	13991	315.1	13732	309.3	3.50	1.18
1962/63	14796	325.9	13994	308.2	1.91	(–) 0.36
1963/64	16975	365.8	14769	318.3	5.54	3.28
1964/65	20000	421.9	15884	335.1	7.55	5.28
1965/66	20636	425.5	15081	310.9	(–) 5.06	(–) 7.22
1966/67	23810	481.0	15257	308.2	1.17	(–) 0.87
1967/68	28166	566.6	16616	328.4	8.91	6.55
1968/69	28859	557.1	17180	331.7	3.39	1.00
1969/70	31968	604.3	18152	343.1	5.66	3.44
1970/71	34627	640.1	19035	351.8	4.86	2.54
1971/72	36599	660.6	19299	348.4	1.39	(–) 0.97
1972/73	39592	698.3	19130	337.4	(–) 0.88	(–) 3.16
1973/74	49290	849.8	19724	340.1	3.11	0.80

Source: Datta et al., 1975, Table 1, p. 1540.

1930/31 and 1948/49 (V.K.R.V. Rao, quoted in Malenbaum, 1962:109).
The average annual per capita income rose from $51.87 in 1948/49 to $120
in 1971, a slight increase in real terms due to rising prices and inflation.
Indian per capita income in terms of 1960/61 prices increased from Rs 257 in
1948/ 49 to Rs 350 in 1973/74, a rise in index from 83.9 to 114.3 (Mukherjee
and Chatterjee, 1974:255). The total net national product grew by an average of 3.48 percent annually between 1951/52 and 1973/74, but in terms of
per capita income the increase was only 1.35 percent (Datta et al., 1975:
Table 2). The latter figure is explained by rapid population growth (about
2.25 percent annually in the last decade).

Indian economic expansion has just barely been able to keep pace with population growth (Cassen, 1978:237). In terms of aspirations and expectations, such annual economic growth can hardly be perceived as capable of significantly reducing strains and frustrations among the poor. The income of nearly sixty percent of the population has been below the national per capita average. Disregarding regional variations, the standard of living has been very low and for most people has not exceeded subsistence even by Indian standards (Bardhan, 1974; S. Basu, 1975; Dandekar and Rath, 1971; Ganguli and Gupta, 1976). The situation was defined by V.K.R.V. Rao in the fifties as a "static economy in progress." This static nature may encourage the belief that the national pie is stable and that the only way to improve one's lot and increase one's share is at the expense of others, hence increasing the potential for conflict and discontent.

The potential for discontent is further reinforced by manifest Indian ideology and formal legislation (B.B. Chatterjee et al., 1971; K.S. Rao, 1973). The egalitarian slogans which have largely dominated politics and the judiciary system have legitimized and encouraged a rise in expectations among the lower classes. This has fed the sense of deprivation and increased strain.

What might further aggravate the situation is the lag between economic growth and structural change in the economy. This may be understood by considering the distribution of gross national product with regard to economic branches over a twenty-three year period. Between 1950/51 and 1973/74 the share of secondary and tertiary sectors rose from 16.0 to 22.4 percent, and from 26.6 to 34.8 percent respectively. Nevertheless, the primary (agricultural) sector continued to dominate the economy, notwithstanding a slight decrease from 57.0 to 42.8 percent over the same period (see Table 3:2). "The most startling feature of the change [was] the failure of the occupational structure to coincide with the sectoral net domestic product structure" (V.K.R.V. Rao, 1979:2049). This means that most of the manpower was not occupationally fluid but rather tied to villages and traditional occupations. This lack of correspondence between the structure of the economy and the occupational distribution of manpower has been another source of discontent.

TABLE 3:2

NET DOMESTIC PRODUCT BY SECTOR
(At Constant Prices)

	Primary Sector	Secondary Sector	Tertiary Sector
1950/51	57.0%	16.4%	26.6%
1960/61	52.2	19.1	28.7
1970/71	45.8	22.1	32.1
1973/74	42.8	22.4	34.8

Source: Datta et al., 1975, Table 4, p. 1543.

In sum, while studies may appear to indicate a degree of economic growth, this has nevertheless been slow in comparison with aspirations, backed by egalitarian ideology. Furthermore, structural change in the economy has not kept pace with even this modest rate of growth. Finally, the slight change that has characterized the economic structure has been accompanied by even less change in occupational distribution and income. These factors collectively impede integration in India.

STRUCTURAL MULTIPLICITY

The coexistence of different (or even antagonistic) behavioral codes within and between social spheres is conducive to social conflict and anomie. In the case of India this structural duality or multiplicity is found in almost all social institutions and spheres. Multiplicity manifests itself in the value system, in family life, in social stratification, and in the legal, political, administrative, educational, and economic spheres.

The Indian value system is officially defined in largely modern, secular constitutional terms and is based on civil concepts of equality, freedom, and individual rights. At the same time, traditional, hierarchical, religious, and non-individual values continue to be major sources of legitimation for most of the Indian population.

Dualism in the family structure is strongly pronounced. The Indian joint family, with authority traditionally vested in the elders, provides a strong contrast to the nuclear family and the increasing autonomy of younger Indians. Consequently, the family has frequently become a cultural battlefield where many factors are focalized. In an attempt to avoid conflict, Indians, especially urban dwellers, adopt a dual behavioral style — one within the family, the other outside it.[1]

Similarly, although the English legal system is supposed to define the normative structure of Indian society, many Hindu and Muslim laws or mores are incorporated into the system and used to settle disputes and regulate behavior (Derrett, 1979). Although India has a well-developed bureaucracy, its universalistic orientation is frequently hampered by traditional obligations (Braibanti, 1963).

In the political sphere multiplicity is reflected by the fact that "closed" caste associations generally act as mobilizing agents in an "open" party system (Rudolph and Rudolph, 1967: Pt.I; Weiner, 1967). Another indicator of political multiplicity is the gap between the universalistic norms of the central elite culture and the particularistic norms of the peripheral mass culture (Weiner, 1965).

Along the same lines, a traditional estate system coexists with a more open patterns of stratification (Gould, 1969). In the economic field a modern market coexists with a redistributive system in which conventional techniques and self-sufficiency prevail.

From the beginning of the twentieth century structural multiplicity has often been utilized by the lower *jatis* for the purpose of mobility, thereby increasing social tension (Beteille, 1974:104). Many *jatis* have used what may be termed a "dual path" pattern of mobility; that is, they have combined ritual sanskritization with their economic, political, and educational resources in order to change their status. This dual pattern of mobility has accentuated primordial and class differences (Srinivas, 1969).

Related to dualism and multiplicity is the increasing structural divergence between institutions. As we shall see in Chapter 8, both political and educational development in India surpass economic development. Despite the large variability within each institutional sphere, one may claim that the use of power is more fluid and widespread than that of economic resources or prestige,[2] primarily because of the relative scarcity and limited change in the economic sphere.

CLASS DIVISION

In this study the class factor is briefly discussed in terms of its weight and relationship to other factors in Indian society. When focusing upon class, three points must be considered: the extent to which socio-economic differences exist, the degree to which these differences have been crystallized into class consciousness and organization, and the dynamics of their articulation in class conflicts (Eisenstadt, 1971).

A brief survey of the situation in Indian society reveals that various groups can be identified and ranked according to their position in the production system, their income, occupation, and education — factors which are highly correlated (Bardhan, 1974; Beteille, 1965; G.S. Chatterjee, 1976; V. Singh, 1973).

A recent review of the patterns of income distribution in India indicates that the ratio between the upper and lower deciles of income is about one to ten, while in urban areas it is even higher. A modest trend towards an increase in this gap has been noted since independence (Bardhan, 1974:104—105). Further, the so-called middle and working classes are quite small (L.K. Sen, 1969).

Both the development of class consciousness and the establishment of class-oriented organizations seem to be rather weak, as may be indicated by the relatively small membership in and support of trade unions (about four million persons) and "leftist" class-oriented parties (about ten percent of the voting population in 1977). It must be noted, however, that a slow process of increased membership is evolving (Karnik, 1966; S. Sen, 1977; G.K. Sharma, 1971). Although articulation of "pure" class interests in both institutional and extra-institutional activities is quite limited, such interests are widely manipulated through the channel of caste or faction.

Another source of antagonism and deprivation is found within classes, especially among the active segments of the society (i.e., the educated) be-cause of low salaries and widespread unemployment. These unemployed and underemployed educated represent a high potential for discontent and strain,[3] which may be accentuated by their position as marginal men torn between East and West (Shils, 1961). Student unrest may be an indicator of this strain (M.P. Reddy, 1969).

Despite the minimal articulation of "pure" class differences, there is a highly explosive potential for class struggle. It has been reported that most laborers are subject to increasing pressures and exploitation, as may be illus-trated by the following example:

Calcutta has about 2,000 sandal-making units employing close to 10,000 workers. In most cases small producers are themselves the laborers. The pro-duction costs for a pair of ordinary sandals cannot be less than Rs 13. Never-theless, the wholesaler's purchasing price for a pair is about Rs 12, while his selling price to the retailer is about Rs 22. The workers survive only because they somehow occasionally manage to make and sell some "fancy" goods or to have individual retail sales. However, in ordinary bulk production, the sandal makers are the perpetual losers. They are caught between the monopoly of the dealers in raw materials and the wholesalers (T. Basu, 1977:1262). The situation has led to increasing tension and strain. It therefore becomes clear that "pure" class division in India is increasingly becoming an independent source of structural strain.

Class and Caste

The potential for disintegration rises considerably due to the congruency of class and caste affiliations.[4] Whenever the legitimacy of the traditional caste hierarchy is challenged, existing socio-economic differences become a source of class conflict. Conversely, whenever the definition of class conflict is extended to include primordial terms, specific disputes usually become more broadly based.

The relationship between class components and caste (relative weight of each and the degree of overlap) varies greatly from region to region. In gen-eral, all the possible logical patterns of relationship between caste and class can be found from full congruence to total compartmentalization. Although from the beginning of the century there has been a perceptible process of increasing divergence between hierarchy of caste and class (Dasgupta and Morris-Jones, 1976:191), at present the relationship between the two is still strong. For example, Bhatt found the correlation between caste and socio-economic status over all of India to be about .35 (1975:74).

Some of the lower castes, especially the harijans, constitute a unique class in economic terms. Dubey and Mathur (1972) have reported that of the 65 million members of the scheduled (untouchable) castes and tribes (comprising about 15 percent of the total Indian population), 90 percent are illiterate.

Lack of education has largely prevented these castes and tribes from attaining economic and political mobility. Their stronger concentration in rural areas has aggravated the problem by giving a geographical flavor to primordial and class differences [*Census of India, 1971*, Series I, India Paper (A.C. Serkhar), Table 1, p. 3].

In general, scholars differ in their analyses of the degree and pattern of congruence between class and caste in India. Dumont, for example, describes a semi-pluralist cross-cutting pattern of stratification (1970:36, 240–258). Beteille, however, tends to evaluate the phenomenon as less pluralistic, stressing the congruence between class and caste (1965). If generalizations can be made at all, one may claim, on the basis of available evidence, that the lower the level of a group or region in socio-economic terms and the stronger its rural element, the greater the overlapping between primordial and class factors (Bhatt, 1975:170–173; Dasgupta and Morris-Jones, 1976:191ff).

Three major pieces of research have dealt with the combination of class and caste elements from the beginning of the century – Kopf (1969) on Bengal, Hardgrave (1969) on Tamil Nadu, and Omvedt (1976) on Maharashtra. All three point to the rise of the Brahmins and other upper castes as new, modern ruling classes in the nineteenth and twentieth centuries and view the revolt of the lower castes against them in caste terms. Despite the differences in geographic areas and groups involved in the clash, most of these studies have come to the conclusion that although class strain is surely embedded in every economic and political conflict, the most important devices used in such clashes are caste associations and coalitions.

There is general agreement that the relationship between caste and socio-economic status was much stronger and of a greater magnitude in the past than in recent years in both rural and urban areas (Beteille, 1965; Bhatt, 1975:73; V. Singh, 1973). The growing incongruence between caste and class, however, has created a situation whereby each affiliation has served as a substitute to or has complemented the other, thus increasing fluidity and accentuating the disintegrative potential (Patil, 1979:289–295).

POLITICAL SPLITS

An additional disintegrative element in the Indian system is the population's division into various competitive political associations and factions (Brass, 1974; Rudolph and Rudolph, 1967), which is further accentuated by its partial congruence with caste and/or class (Dasgupta and Morris-Jones, 1976; Weiner, 1975). In 1975 Bhatt reported that the correlation between caste and political participation for all of India and specifically for the rural areas was .11, while in the urban areas it was .04; the highly stratified states of Uttar Pradesh and West Bengal showed a correlation of .13 and .18 respectively (1975:126). With socio-economic status held constant, the correlation between various indicators of political activity and caste strongly decline

(Bhatt, 1975:137). Dasgupta and Morris-Jones have shown that the level of socio-economic development is strongly correlated (.83) with valid votes (1976:71). This finding may indicate the increasing potential of class conflict in political terms. However, by no means can one find full impingement of class upon politics (Dasgupta and Morris-Jones, 1976:187).

On the local level, especially in rural areas, caste serves as a nucleus for both class and political groupings (Bharati, 1976; Carter, 1974; Lynch, 1976; Walch, 1976). In general, politics can be described as a divisive factor, which accentuates the strain between primordial and non-primordial factors and serves as a focal point for over-all social antagonisms (Bharati, 1976; Crane, 1976). In this sense, political maneuvering becomes a basis for political (power-oriented) stratification (Carter, 1974). At the same time, because of its structure, Indian politics is used to institutionalize splits and conflicts.

Political mobilization of primordial sentiments and class interests is frequently undertaken on a regional or even national level (Crane, 1976). Lynch, for example, has shown how Dravidian sentiments impinging upon class differences in Bombay were politically aggregated and utilized for economic and occupational purposes, thus increasing class struggles in the city (1976: 24–25). Politics often serves as a focal point for sentiments, religious beliefs, socio-economic interests, and ideologies (Bharati, 1976).

Having pointed out the high potential for clash between class factions, primordial elements, and politics, let us deal with the degree and pattern in which such a conflict is actualized.

Strains based upon a degree of overlap between socio-economic interests and primordial factors have been common in India since at least the beginning of the century (Aiyar, 1976; A.R. Desai, 1954). These tensions are usually described in connection with the rise of new patterns of social organization, such as unions, peasant associations, *zamindari* bodies, and political factions. To some extent, their increasing potential for conflict has been linked to twentieth-century liberal reforms introduced by the British and to the emergence of Indian nationalism. In the early 1900s Chirol (1910) wrote about Indian unrest, his main thesis being that the emergence of an open arena for competition and the increase of fluid groups due to economic, legal, and political change would add weight to strains and conflicts. He predicted that the combination of several factors, such as class interests, rising aspirations, a sense of deprivation, communal sentiments, and political associations, would make unrest and conflict in India almost unbearable. His analysis of various "symptoms" of discontent, such as the Hindu revival, student unrest, and the revolt of the depressed castes, shows how explosive he perceived the situation to be.

Legal and political reforms equalizing the position of all classes increased Indian potential for class conflict. New universal rules and political organizations provided tools with which to manipulate class interests and offered a basis for their legitimation. The various political reforms which ended in the diarchy (double government) and home rule in the late thirties legitimized wider representation. Under these conditions, different types of groups (castes, religious groups, classes) attempted to mobilize their resources and convert them into power, prestige, and economic assets. This process resulted in a steady increase in the number, intensity, and violence of socio-political clashes (Ghosh, 1975; Ranga, 1949).

The severity of the conflict potential inherent in combined class and political differences can be illustrated by two violent affairs. The first case, the Telangana revolt (late forties to early fifties), was directed against the nizam of Hyderabad and his feudal methods and sought to gain redistribution of land and "people's rule" (Sundarayya, 1972). It was led by the Communist Party of India (CPI), which succeeded in mobilizing mass support and transforming the struggle into a peasant war. During the period between 1947 and 1950 the rebels established their political dominancy in some parts of Telangana, seizing and distributing land to poor peasants. The movement was finally crushed by the Indian army at the end of 1950. According to Communist sources, about 4,000 people were killed and 10,000 jailed after the suppression. These figures may indicate the scope of the revolt (Dhanagare, 1974).

The second case concerns the Naxalite movement, which was launched in 1967 in West Bengal and Andhra Pradesh and declined in the beginning of the 1970s. Its aim was to force land redistribution by demolishing the "oppressing" institutions of the establishment and seizing State power (B. Dasgupta, 1974; Ghosh, 1975; A.K. Roy, 1975). As in the Telangana revolt, the movement was led by the Marxist-Leninist segment of the Communist party. In its infancy (1967), the movement's activities were characterized by almost spontaneous, sporadic outbreaks in the rural areas of West Bengal. These uprisings did not crystallize into strong associations until April 1969, when an attempt was made by the CPI (Marxists) to organize and politicize the movement, causing the clashes between different strata of peasants to become accentuated. At this stage it became clear that many of the participants were not interested in the ideological aspects or long-term goals of the movement but rather sought to improve their immediate position. Thus, in many instances the Naxalites' actions were hardly different from those of criminal elements. This enabled the police to counter-attack with violent, extra-legal tactics, and the Naxalites, in turn, became more violent and anti-institutional. With the accentuation of clashes in 1969, the movement spread to the urban areas and the student population became involved. The widening scope of the movement threatened the ruling classes, which implemented increasingly harsher measures to crush the revolts, including the enforcement of presidential rule in West Bengal (1971). Such repressive measures brought an end to the movement, at least officially.

While neither the Naxalite movement nor the Telangana revolt ever developed into a real revolution, their very occurrence indicates that the structural combination of class, caste, and politics is conducive to strain and enables mobilization of the masses in the name of both a generalized belief and particularistic interests.[5]

THE RURAL-URBAN GAP

Yet another non-primordial source of potential strains relates to the gap between India's urban and rural areas. About eighty percent of the population lives in rural areas and twenty percent in urban areas.[6] The twenty-percent urbanization rate has not changed significantly since the beginning of the century.

A number of factors have aggravated this situation. Firstly, large parts of the rural periphery see the urban population as a reference group. Secondly, the cities have become a center of gravitation for the most mobile parts of the rural population. Thirdly, the power of decision, policy-making, and resources are concentrated in the cities, while most clients live in the villages. Lastly, the conflict potential within both sectors, increased by social change, has strongly impinged on the relationship between the two areas. To understand the various underlying factors of the geographical-social split, let us briefly analyze conditions in each sector.

Despite the variation in Indian rural patterns and different scholarly approaches to the subject, it is possible to delineate some characteristics common to Indian villages (Dube, 1955; Kessinger, 1974; Marriott, 1968; Oommen, 1977; Wiser and Wiser, 1971).

The majority of the village population is at an elementary level of subsistence and, in relation to aspirations (and by definition), is greatly deprived. Moreover, income is quite unequally distributed so that some parts of the village population have a much higher revenue than others. In addition, the post-independence legal and political attempts at land redistribution and the abolition of various types of landlordism (i.e., *zamindari, kyotwari,* and *talugdari*) have actually increased the potential for conflict in the Indian village (B. Singh, 1961 : Ch. II).

Although the *zamindari* groups differ from area to area in terms of caste, they have been able to mobilize power on the regional level as a class. Since the beginning of the century the Landlords' Party and various local *zamindari* associations have used their economic power and Hindu communal symbols to legitimize their position and to counter demands of the poor peasants and lower castes (Reeves, 1976: CH.III, Stockes, 1976). Since independence the trend has been continuing and has even been accentuated (Brass, 1965: Ch. IV, Junankar, 1975).

The attempts to redistribute land have legitimized the poor peasants' demands for legal and political change, providing them with an adequate tool with which to fight their landlords. Since the beginning of the century there have been increasing indications of the rise of peasant associations (B.B. Chatterjee et al., 1971) and lower-caste interest groups, perhaps the best example being the Anti-Brahmin Movement in Madras of the 1920s. The rise of such organizations may be partially responsible for increasing violent clashes in rural India (Ranga, 1949; Stockes, 1976). Improvements in agricultural methods have also widened the socio-economic gaps (Laxminarayan, 1977). There is evidence that areas in which the Green Revolution was successful showed increased signs of inequality – and of clashes (Junankar, 1975).

The combined factors of population growth, improved cultivation methods, and the shortage of alternative job opportunities in industry created a free-floating proletariat (A. Sen, 1975), a process which has been evident from the early 1950s. For example, the *Reports of the Committees of the Panel on Land Reforms* show that at that time 22 percent of rural householders had no land and 75 percent had five acres or less (1956:3). Dandekar and Rath (1971) report that about 30 percent of rural households were non-cultivating in the 1960s, while a more recent survey estimates the proportion to be about 47 percent (Vyas and Bandyopadhyay, 1975: Table 4, A-5). The phenomenon of free-floating manpower has had a number of consequences. For one, the fact that landless laborers are sometimes economically better off than small landowners (Patnaik, 1976) has increased their capacity to organize and confront the upper classes on the village level.

Since the beginning of the twentieth century, if not earlier, the opportunity for active segments of the population to migrate to urban areas has been enhanced. A study by Dasgupta and Laishley (1975), based on data about forty Indian villages, found that migrants from the villages originated from the more mobile parts of the population. Thus, literacy is higher among the migrants than among the average villagers, and it is the higher castes, rather than the lower, that tend to move to urban areas. If this is true, it means that a process of "negative" selection, whereby rural areas are deprived of the most active sections of their population, is occurring. Consequently, there has been an increase in the gap between rural and urban areas.

The increase in manpower fluidity is usually accompanied by an increasing number of caste associations competing for political leadership (Bailey, 1960; Carter, 1974). This has turned the battle over the control of resources in the rural areas into a more organized, collective-oriented confrontation. For example, research of rural Maharashtra has shown that traditional factional conflicts have been reinforced by competition for control of modern enterprises, such as milk cooperatives, and for the resources allocated by various governmental programs (Westergaard et al., 1976:162).

With regard to urban India there is general agreement among scholars that it consists of a wider variety of cultures and structures than what is common in the West (Bose, 1973; Fox, 1970a). There is also agreement that Indian patterns of urbanization are by no means parallel to Western ones (M.S.A. Rao, 1970, 1974). There is, however, disagreement among scholars about the nature of India's urbanization process (Bose, 1965; Saberwal, 1976). Some think that it essentially entails a mere transfer of population and does not mark a real cultural and political transformation; others describe the cities as a mixture of urban and rural patterns, and still others claim that large sections of Indian cities are indeed urban in their social pattern.

Despite the variation in research findings and interpretations or opinions, it seems valid to claim that most Indian cities are in a transitional stage and are composed of both urban and rural elements (what M.S.A. Rao called "rurban") or that the cities are structured in various forms of "dualism" (Rosenthal, 1976). This is also true with regard to many of India's larger villages. Trivedi (1976) has revealed that many small towns were classified as rural settlements in the 1961 census although their occupational structure was non-rural; that is, about 75 percent of their inhabitants were engaged in non-agricultural work. In general, Indian towns and cities can be described as rurban, or may be viewed as made up of clusters of rural and urban elements in different proportions. This mixture of rural and urban often leads to anomie and therefore increases the explosive potential in both cities and towns. The uniqueness of the urban phenomenon (speaking in terms of the "ideal type" to include both cities and towns) is its combination of antagonistic and undifferentiated sets of codes and frameworks and its make-up of a mixture of isolated groups (M.S.A. Rao, 1974:97ff). Theoretically, this structure can be viewed as a specific pattern of divergence which exists within each institutional sphere, such as the economy or the family, and not only among them.

Indian urban structures and values have generally been somewhere between tradition and modernity. Despite their tremendous growth, there is no indication of a great difference between the so-called pre-industrial and industrial cities, all of them being structurally dual (Fox, 1969b, 1970a, 1970b). This can be illustrated in various social spheres. For example, the old *jati* ascriptive-oriented principles of stratification coexist with a new class criteria based on achievement and wealth; old communal identities coexist with more universal national ones; and patrimonial political affiliations coexist with more open associations.

The transfer of rural migrants to the cities without adequate provision of economic and social facilities for their absorption has increased the urban potential for explosive discontent and anomie (Bose, 1973; Kulkarni, 1976). Since the poorest and most frustrated parts of the population, as well as the most privileged classes, are concentrated in specific parts of the cities, the differences become even more salient, leading to a face-to-face confrontation (Dasgupta and Laishley, 1975). Further, since the poorest echelon frequently contains the most active migrants, such a confrontation often evolves into a violent clash.

Indian cities are composed of collectivities: joint families or groups, rather than individuals. Urban dwellers are usually affiliated with dominant groups which do not overlap in a pluralistic way, but rather live parallelly, mixed only to a certain degree. The relative stability of the groups, which stems from a shortage of occupational opportunities and little chance of mobility, reinforces the primordial measures of prestige (Fox, 1969b:Ch.5). This means that many of the clashes in the cities occur between groups rather than individuals, the result of three main factors: the relative blurring of traditional boundaries, the increasing fluidity of traditional groups, and an increase in competition among them. Under such conditions, the slightest agitation between individuals may provoke a clash between groups. The force of this explosive potential may be illustrated by the riots which erupted in Rourkela, Orissa in March 1964. With an influx of refugees from East Pakistan, the "objective" potential for tension was increased, and a spread of rumors was transformed into a violent clash between the main primordial groups of the city (Hindus, Muslims, and Adivasis) (V.B. Chatterjee et al., 1957:33–36).

The issue is further complicated because most Indian urban elites hold a marginal position; that is, they have to operate under the cross-pressure of antagonistic codes. Generally this may have a paralyzing effect, limiting the leadership's capacity to construct institutional mechanisms with which to cope with conflicts. Again the potential for strain – within both rural and urban sectors – is consequently raised.

The gap between the villages and cities may be said to contain four partially overlapping aspects. The first is its high correlation with the gap between the traditional periphery and the modern centers (although there are traditional enclaves in cities and modern enclaves in the rural areas) (Weiner, 1965). This difference can easily be transformed into a legitimacy gap.

Second, the rural areas lag behind the urban in terms of standard of living. The average income in rural areas in 1968 was about Rs 250 per capita, whereas in urban areas it was Rs 356 (Dandekar and Rath, 1971:25–29). Furthermore, income distribution is more equal within rural than within urban areas (Bardhan, 1974; Ojha and Bhatt, 1964). This gap can easily be perceived in terms of unfair distribution of justice and not only economic deprivation.

The third aspect is education: the illiteracy rate of the rural population is eighty percent as opposed to forty percent among the urban population. This gulf decreases the opportunities for peaceful communication between the two sectors.

The gap is less salient regarding the fourth aspect, the political sphere, but it is still wide enough to influence the conflict potential. While the village has grown politically stronger, most of the decision-making power remains concentrated in the city.

Analysis of India's rural and urban areas has shown that the potential for conflict within and between both areas has been strengthened by the increasing social fluidity and interdependence. As the relationship between urban and rural sectors has become more symmetrical, the tensions between them have also increased (Weintraub, 1970).

STRAINED UNION-STATES RELATIONSHIPS

India is composed of a federation or union of twenty-two states and seven union territories. Although the relationships between these states and the Indian Union are legally and politically institutionalized, in actuality, there is continual friction between them as well as among the states themselves (Maheshwari, 1973). Essentially, the situation can be described as a struggle between centrifugal and centripetal tendencies. The unsuccessful attempts from the period of British rule to unify the Princely states, provinces, and various autonomous cultural and political territories into one socio-political entity have often accentuated these strains.

Three basic sources of tension have been noted. First, there are usually linguistic, racial, and cultural differences among the states. For example, the principal languages of Andhra Pradesh are Telugu and Urdu; in Assam, Bengali; in Haryana, Hindi; in Maharashtra, Navathi; in Orissa, Oriya; and in Punjab, Punjabi. Along the same lines, the Bengali "race" and culture differs from that of Maharashtra. Sometimes religion also divides certain states, as is the case between the Sikhs of Punjab and the Hindus of Haryana.

A second source of friction is the difference in standard of living; in other words, some states are better off economically than others.[7] For example, comparing the richest and poorest states in 1972, the ratio between their per capita income was approximately two to one; the difference in public expenditure for the same year was three to one; and the ratio of per capita federal transfer of funds was two to one (K.N. Reddy, 1976). A distinction is also made between surplus and shortage states. The former (e.g., Tamil Nadu and Punjab) produce more than is needed, the latter (Bengal and Bihar) produce less. This economic gap forces the central authority to intervene in such matters as the allocation of grain and other foodstuffs and in the fixing of prices.

Because of extremely limited resources, the allocation of Union funds to the states is accompanied by heated disputes each year, and the center is ultimately forced to find a compromise between conflicting demands. One state often benefits at the expense of another, and this quasi zero-sum relationship accentuates the strains among the states and between them and the center. The conflict is often sharpened by internal pressures between various interest groups within each state (Fox, 1971; M.S.A. Rao, 1977). In this way, internal politics influence national politics and Union-state relationships.

Strain has also resulted from the effort of local politicians to develop political autonomy, generally through the manipulation of both primordial sentiments and socio-economic interests. This situation has often made it difficult for central politicians to operate cohesive political parties. Hence, many confrontations are between small bargaining bodies, making clashes more acute and anomic in nature.

On several occasions the interpretation of inter-state political issues at an intra-party level has led to conflict between the central government and the states. Local branches of the ruling party have sometimes attempted to take over a state in which they did not enjoy a majority. An example of such is the case of West Bengal, where the ruling center utilized laws and organs of the Indian Union several times since 1967 to enforce presidential rule. In other cases, the ruling center has favored certain states economically to assure their dominancy, thereby causing deprivation in other states. On the whole, relations between the center and the states have often become subject to political bargaining, with its accompanying strain (Maheshwari, 1973).

CONCLUSIONS

The past two chapters have been directed towards a delineation of India's high potential for disintegration in terms of structural duality, primordial and non-primordial diversity, and scarcity (economic deprivation). In theoretical terms, the diversity we have described indicates a large potential for social polarization and the focalization of conflict, where most of the conflicts involve value and norm components and are not confined to the organizational level.

The dynamics of social unity in India may be described on a very general level as characterized by declining ascriptive loyalties and increasing functional affiliations, that is, grouping according to occupational interests, income, and the like. This development dates back to the beginning of the present century and has become much more prominent in recent years. Nonetheless, the congruence between functional positions and primordial elements is still very strong; primordial factors are central in determining the boundaries of conflicts, probably because they are one of the least expensive units for mobilizing power. As a result, primordial factors have often been utilized as a vehicle for class interests and struggle, rather than the other way around (Ghurye, 1968). The cost of mobilizing class interests and voting power in primordial associations may be very high in terms of disintegration since it may perpetuate social splits on both the symbolic and organizational levels. Furthermore, the manipulation of primordial sentiments in open economic and political markets makes the division much more prominent.

The various disintegrative factors discussed here are manipulated almost everywhere in India, but the level on which they operate and their relative weight and composition differ from region to region. Thus, the *jati* division as combined with class differences is most important on the village level, while on a broader local level religious or caste differences are strongly manipulated. In urban centers class division is of great importance. The above splits are reinforced by increasing political fluidity and redistribution of power, which is accompanied by minor change in the redistribution of wealth. The intensity of this structural divergence further accentuates the potential for conflict.

Complementing the above process is the existence in almost every institutional sphere of different or even antagonistic codes of behavior. In both primordial and functional terms the Indian patterns of division seem to be acute. This split refers not only to the problem of distance, polarization, and focalization but also to the gap between values and reality. Furthermore, under conditions of scarcity, when large parts of the population live at a substandard level, the relationships among the various groups can easily be transformed into zero-sum relationships.[8]

Despite all these factors and contrary to various predictions of a breakdown (Harrison, 1960), Indian society has shown a remarkable ability to absorb conflicts and to institutionalize them. This cannot be explained away by mass apathy, fatalism, or the use of naked force. How, then, does one explain India's capacity to manage its social system with almost fully democratic means in such a way that both its basic legitimacy and integration have been preserved, to a certain degree, over the last thirty-two years?

In essense, the remainder of this book will attempt to demonstrate that although the divisive factors described above increase conflicts, they have been structured in a way that has enabled them to institutionalize disputes, thereby maintaining the unity of Indian society.

NOTES

1. See, for example, Kapadia, 1959, 1966; D. Narain, 1975; Nimkoff, 1959.

2. In every institutional sphere socio-economic variables vary highly from state to state (Dasgupta and Morris-Jones, 1976:68–71), a fact which may indicate the structural divergence in the Indian system. However, the relationship between this set of variables and political participation is more consistent, the rank correlations between development (an index of 24 socio-economic variables) and participation in elections (valid votes) being high (.88) (Dasgupta and Morris-Jones, 1976:71). This, nevertheless, cannot be considered an indicator of structural convergence. Rather, it indicates that on the average Indian political fluidity lags behind socio-economic fluidity. Such a political development has encouraged various poor, non-educated groups to utilize their power. Since this move has not been backed by wealth or prestige, the result has been "political inflation" where there is too much power chasing too little wealth.

3 See Blaug et al., 1969: *Report of the Committee on Unemployment,* 1973.

4. For a recent systematic discussion on class and caste in India, see *Economic and Political Weekly,* Vol. XIV, Annual Number (February 1979).

5. For the use of these terms, see Smelser's theory of collective behavior (1962, 1968:96–99).

6. Urban areas in India include all locations with a minimum population of 5,000 where at least 75 percent of the employed male population is involved in non-agricultural work and the population density is at least 400 per square kilometer. (*Statistical Abstract of the India Union, 1972,* Table 1, p. 3).

7. Dasgupta and Morris-Jones (1976) divide the states according to nine "developing" variables: per capita income, literacy, retail trade, manufacturing, percentage of immigrants, electricity, factories, percentage of farmers in rural areas, and percentage of rural population (the first seven are negatively correlated with the latter two). The correlation coefficients range from .30 to .93, but only in four out of twenty-one cases are they below .50 (Dasgupta and Morris-Jones, 1976:50). With these consistent socio-economic

differences and despite the regional differences within states, Dasgupta and Morris-Jones were able to grade the states in the following order: Punjab, Kerala, Tamil Nadu, and West Bengal at the top; Maharashtra and Mysore in the middle; and Bihar and Ragastam at the bottom (1976:14).

8. There is another possible interpretation. Under conditions of scarcity, the shortage of food, money, and employment could lead to extremely obedient and conformist behavior because most people are afraid of losing their small share of the national pie. This interpretation sees Indian integration as "negative," i.e., based on the assumption that it is better to survive in bad conditions than to try to work toward change. However, as will be shown below, Indian integration is essentially based on "positive" factors.

Chapter 4

SYNTHESIS OF TRADITIONAL AND MODERN
PATTERNS OF INTEGRATION

INTRODUCTION

In order to understand how Indian society has coped with its divisive elements it is necessary to analyze the traditional patterns of integration, their decline, and the transformation of old concepts into modern approaches to integration.

Social integration refers to a society's capacity to use institutional mechanisms in dealing with social conflict and deprivation. Extrapolating from the general assumption that several options of achieving social legitimation and integration are available, we can assume that societies tend to choose those alternatives most beneficial and least expensive to most of their members, or at least to their strongest segments.

It is generally the elites, ruling classes, or most powerful groups in society which select a certain pattern of legitimation and integration. When the ruling elites maintain their social position for a relatively long time, their interests are often crystallized and translated into traditional patterns of behavior. Substantial social change, however, raises doubts about the expediency of the traditional system and also endangers the position of the elites. The course taken by the ruling center under such circumstances will largely depend upon their resources.

In India, with the encounter between colonial and indigenous powers, the traditional system gradually declined. Consequently, the educated elites saw it in their interests to manipulate tradition, integrating the old and the new into one system. This pattern of integration, which aimed at maximizing stability while promoting social change, essentially reflected both the power (i.e., resources) and interests of the upper strata. These groups manipulated the social system on both the symbolic and the institutional level so as to minimize anomic or revolutionary trends and to maintain their privileged position.

The present chapter, in describing this manipulation, first reveals the basic elements of the traditional patterns of integration, then deals with their erosion, and finally considers their reconstruction in modern terms.

ELEMENTS IN THE TRADITIONAL PATTERN OF LEGITIMATION AND INTEGRATION

In discussing the traditional pattern of legitimation and integration, we refer to an almost "ideal type" of order which dominated Hindu society until the beginning of the eighteenth century (see Weber, 1958).

The Indian traditional pattern of integration can be described as the dialectical combination of primordial and functional elements, transcendental and pragmatic aspects, and continuity (non-change) and dynamic change. The first dialectic set was evident in the specific Indian pattern of division of labor. Primordial elements contributed to a sense of homogeneity and similarity within each unit, while a system of occupational specialization linked social units. Various primordial groups were thereby functionally combined and a special type of interdependence developed.

To illustrate the operation of this dialectic framework, four patterns of integration are described: the *varna* system (interlinking among castes), sanskritization and the doctrine of transmigration (among *varnas*), the *jajmani* system (among sub-castes, i.e., *jatis*) and the *jati panchayat* network (within *jatis*).

The Varna *System*

The most important element in the traditional pattern of integration was the *varna* (caste) system. Indian society was divided into four major *varnas* traditionally defined in terms of broad occupational categories and ranked accordingly: (1) the Brahmins, the priestly and learned class; (2) the Kshatriyas, the military and governing class; (3) the Vaishyas, traders and cattle raisers; and (4) the Shudras, the servants and menial laborers of the three higher castes. Outside the *varna* system were the ritually impure outcastes or untouchables – the lowest scheduled classes of Hindu society.

Each *varna*, as well as the outcastes, was sub-divided into local *jatis*, largely autonomous units in the sense that each had its own regulations for marriage, religious rituals, and other matters. *Jatis* were ranked according to their *varna* status, specific occupational functions, wealth, and land ownership. In effect, most upper *jatis* were part of the upper *varnas*, and the lower *jatis*, part of the lower *varnas* (Hutton, 1963; O'Malley, 1974; Senart, 1975; Srinivas, 1962), although there were numerous cases of inconsistency between *jati* rank and occupation or wealth (discussed below).

Of interest to our present discussion is the relationship between levels of the *varna* system. The particularistic local *jatis* combined into supra-local caste clusters (an aggregate of persons usually in the same linguistic region, usually with the same traditional occupations, and sometimes with the same caste name; see Bailey, 1963). On the next level some divergent *jatis* with common status constituted regional *varna* categories. Finally, a *varna* scheme organized according to the four-fold traditional classification prevailed on the national level. Thus, the more particularistic levels (local castes) were gradually incorporated into a national, universalistic system, which has given India a sense of unity (Fox, 1969a). This pattern of linkage, however, was rather problematic on the pragmatic level because of the high potential for conflict in daily life.

The Transmigration Doctrine and Sanskritization

Two mechanisms were operated to mitigate the potential strain on the pragmatic level and to absorb it into the system. The transmigration doctrine (*samsara*) aimed at shifting the conflict to the transcendental sphere. Sanskritization acted as an institutionalized safety valve.

The transmigration doctrine had many versions but basically referred to a belief in a cycle of rebirths whereby one's chances of being reborn into a more favorable status improved with full commitment to present duties and functions (W.N. Brown, 1966). This idea was unique to the *varna* system in the sense that it rationalized the permanency of the functional hierarchy (Singer, 1972:45). It did so by connecting this world to the other world, minimizing the possibility of escape from the former by providing transcendental justification to the given reality. In other words, the belief operated as a mechanism by which present circumstances were legitimized by an assumption relating to the unearthly future.

What made the transmigration doctrine system effective was its crystallization into various rituals which linked daily habits with transcendental dimensions. For instance, foods eaten by one *jati* were considered impure for another, but all *jatis* were interdependent in terms of food production (Khare, 1976:151).

The ritualization of daily habits had two consequences, both of which enhanced the legitimacy of the *varna* system. First, it reinforced the institutionalization of caste differences. Second, it reduced the divergence between the symbolic and behavioral levels by combining them dialectically (Mandelbaum, 1966; Marriott, 1976:123ff), a situation which greatly contributed to the legitimacy and integration of traditional Indian society.

Integration was further reinforced by sanskritization, a dynamic mechanism which linked *varna* and *jati* levels. It enabled "a low caste, tribal, or other group, to change its customs, rituals, ideology, and way of life in the direction of a high and frequently twice-born caste" (Srinivas, 1969:6). In its traditional form sanskritization provided a quasi-legitimate mechanism for collective mobility through which the position of an entire *jati* was changed. While wealth was a precondition for status change, ritual was also a factor. In this sense, transcendental and pragmatical levels were interlinked.

Sanskritization provided a means of mobility without endangering the basic premises and "rules" of the caste system. It thus functioned as a shock-absorber, drawing dissenters into the mainstream. In this way, a mechanism with the potential to operate as an anti-system was transformed into an important channel for an institutionalized pattern of social change which reinforced continuity (Alexander, 1968; Srinivas, 1969:7).

The Jajmani *System*

The permanency of the relationships between the units within the caste system was ensured by the *jajmani* system, a specific pattern of hereditary patronage operated as a permanent exchange mechanism among *jatis* (rather than individuals). The system can be understood as a combination of "mechanical" and "organic" elements. It was based on an imbalanced exchange between differential groups whose function and social status were primordially determined.

The two bases of the system were caste status and land ownership. The *jajman* (patron), who usually owned a great deal of land, was generally of upper-caste origin. He was responsible to a *kamin* or *kam karnewala* (client), who belonged to a lower *jati* and performed menial services for his patron (Beidelman, 1959:6-7); Benson, 1976; Breman, 1974:65-67; Kolenda, 1963).

The obligations of the *jajman* to his *kamin* had a balancing effect; that is, they made the transaction between them more reciprocal. As reciprocity increased, so did the legitimacy of the patron and of the system as a whole.

The traditional *jajmani* system gave the *kamins* some bargaining power. Because of the rigid rules governing the division of labor, backed by rituals defining exchange in terms of purity and pollution, upper-caste *jajmans* were dependent on lower-caste *kamins* for certain services. In addition, different castes were dominant in different fields. A caste dominant in ritual would not often be so in either the economic or the political arena (Srinivas, 1969: Ch. I). Along the same lines, a poor Brahmin, for example, could be considered a *kamin* in the religious sense (because he gave services) but a *jajman* in the economic sense (because he accepted services). Such status inconsistencies mitigated the asymmetry of interchange between *jatis*. Some equalization of status was also made possible by the availability of different and sometimes competitive methods of exchange (Mandelbaum, 1970).

Traditionally, however, the interchange among *jatis* was fixed and based on their occupational expertise. Each *jati* was tied to specific functions so that they were related in an almost "organic pattern" (in Durkheim's sense) of primordial division of labor. Hence, the *jajman* relationship included particularistic criteria for transaction within a universally defined exchange system. It must be noted, however, that particularistic affiliations, while given universal meaning, were never fused; rather, the *jajman* utilized his authority in a particularistic way with respect to different clients affiliated with different *jatis.*

The *jajmani* system also differentially connected conditional, voluntaristic, contractual relationships with quasi-compulsive, non-contractual ones. Hypothetically, the *kamin* could choose his *jajman* and transfer from a contractual to a non-contractual relationship (Mandelbaum, 1970:162). However, there was no way to fuse the two and a choice had to be made between them. Free choice was actually very limited in traditional India, not only because of caste and religious boundaries but also because of economic scarcity. Hence, as a rule, limited economic opportunities reduced the bargaining power of the *kamins* so that most *jajmani* relationships were based on quasi-legal unconditional codes.

In light of the above, it is no wonder that with the increasing colonial intervention the *jajmani* system began to decline. This process was reinforced by such factors as population growth, the development of a market-oriented economy, and the increased availability of alternative (non-traditional) jobs, all of which induced workers to seek employment outside their traditional occupations. The result was increased fluidity.

While these changes have sometimes been perceived as narrowing the power gap between *jajmans* and *kamins* (Beidelman, 1959), the opposite was often the case. The surplus of manpower actually reduced the bargaining power of *kamins* and enabled *jajmans* to use *kamin* services in a more exploitative, less obligatory manner (Benson, 1976; Breman, 1974:219). It is true, however, that the development of competitive politics and educational opportunities made for a more egalitarian relationship:

> The members of almost every jati are becoming increasingly diversified in occupations, education, income, and residence. Such diversities have long existed within jatis but they are now more consequential than before.
>
> Villagers continue to see their local social order as being made up of ranked, interdependent jatis but they are revising the criteria for the ranking and the meaning of inter-dependence. The former jajmani relations have lately been much curtailed. Families of different jatis remain dependent on each other economically and frequently also ritually and politically, but the dependence is neither so great nor so mandatory as it was in the past century (Mandelbaum, 1970:655-656).

With the increased openness which developed in the *jajmani* relationship, the power of the system diminished.

The Jati Panchayat

The decline of the *jajmani* system did not affect the status of the *jati* as a collective entity. The power of the latter was perpetuated by virtue of its internal organization. The *jati* council or *panchayat* institution filled an important role in this respect.

In actuality, there were two types of *panchayats*. The village *panchayat* acted as a customary court based on traditional mores combined with executive power. It in turn was composed of a number of *jati panchayats* (often representing only the upper *jatis*). The latter regulated relationships and exchange among families within the *jati* and represented the collective in inter-*jati* matters (Dumont, 1970:174). This dual function gave the *jati panchayat* enormous power, enabling it to become a major tool (exploited under modern conditions) for both maintaining stability and initiating change (Dumont, 1970:77).

To a large extent, efficient operation of the *varna* scheme, the transmigration doctrine, sanskritization, and the *jajmani* system was dependent on the strength and efficiency of the *panchayat*. It was only by virtue of the *jati panchayat* that the universalistic and the particularistic, the transcendental and the pragmatic, and the primordial and the functional were fused and translated into institutional behavior. On the whole, the traditional patterns described above, containing both structural rigidity and flexible elements, had the potential for accommodation to changing circumstances.

THE EROSION AND TRANSFORMATION OF THE TRADITIONAL PATTERN OF INTEGRATION

Under Moghul rule the Indian communal patterns of integration were scarcely touched. There were mechanisms within each community (e.g., Hindu, Muslim) to cope with internal conflict and strain, while disputes between communities were traditionally handled by state intervention, the institutions of the nizam and the maharajahs, or by the central Moghul institutions. In that sense, there was a partial differentiation between state and society.

With the British conquest, new societal concepts and codes of behavior were introduced which greatly contradicted common Indian codes. During the East India Company rule institutional penetration of the traditional system of control was actually slight. However, with the transition from Company to Crown, the British created more and more legal and administrative institutions to maintain order and to defend their interests (Sovani, 1965; Spear, 1965).

Because of this institutional development, structural duality was intensified and clashes between state and local community often resulted. Consequently, the efficiency of the traditional integrative mechanisms for dealing with internal conflicts was reduced. The new institutions constituted alternatives to the traditional channels, thereby increasing disputes, legitimizing caste conflicts, and enabling the lower classes to bargain legally with the dominant castes. In other words, the mere existence of such alternative institutions legitimized new patterns of caste interaction so that some elements of traditional solidarity were shaken (Ghurye, 1969; Kothari, 1970a; Mandelbaum, 1970:307–308; Srinivas, 1969).

Under these conditions Indian society became more fluid and the position of the dominant castes was threatened. The new ruling and educated classes – belonging mostly to the upper castes – were no longer able to fully exploit the traditional pattern of integration. This led them to redefine the concept so as to benefit from both the traditional and modern worlds; that is, they were interested in legitimizing a new pattern of integration in old terms. For this purpose, the traditional concept of social harmony was reinterpreted to take on a more pluralistic pattern.

In utilizing the concept of harmony the educated elites selectively reconsidered and reconstructed certain elements of the past. Essentially, most of the magical and mystical features were eliminated and a distinction was made between the transcendental and pragmatic. On the transcendental level the traditional concept of harmony was maintained, enabling the definition of India as a united society. Pragmatically, however, harmony was redefined as cooperation among equal but interdependent groups having different cultures and occupations. It was in this way that Indian diversity was legitimized and became a basis for unity. The assumption was that while each group (*jati*, ethnic, and linguistic) developed its own identity and unique characteristics, egalitarian cooperation among them was based on mutual dependence. They were able to cooperate because of the consensual transcendental premises which created boundaries for each specific transaction. On this basis both cooperation and bargaining were legitimized.

In the bargaining process conflicting forces competed freely without contractual limitations although within an institutional arena for negotiations. Concepts of equality and competition were therefore embodied into a new notion of harmony.

One of the basic traditional texts used to legitimize this new concept of harmony was the Bhagavadgita. Although their purposes differed, both Tilak and Gandhi selected it as the most acceptable traditional source for effecting direct action in the present.[1] The Bhagavadgita was usually perceived as stressing self-harmony and self-control, qualities mainly dependent upon internal spiritual unity. The true progress of man on earth was perceived as the development of an inner vision, of moral and spiritual action (Bhagavadgita, 1962:35).[2] At the end of the text harmonic spiritual ideas were translated into institutional terms, demanding from each man the attainment of perfection, defined in terms of the traditional *jati* function (Ch.18:41–45). However, modern interpretation of the Gita has somewhat denied the rationale for the original division of society into four *varnas* and "unequivocally asserted the virtual equality of these divisions" (Ghurye, 1969:65). This was the direction taken by both Tilak and Gandhi in their reinterpretations of the text.

Tilak's reinterpretation was first published in Marathi in 1915 and is considered one of the most important attempts to reconstruct Indian tradition. To him the Gita was a philosophy of action similar to modern Western philosophies and therefore applicable to the new conditions in India. He attempted to interpret the text "in order to give philosophical advice as to how one should live one's worldly life," and to reduce the gap between the transcendental and the pragmatic spheres in Indian society. The transcendental aspect provided a symbolic basis for unification, while peaceful interaction between groups was made pragmatical by the unselfish morality and self-restraint embodied in tradition (Tilak, 1935; XLIL, LV, 105).

In his translation of the Gita into Gujarati, Gandhi attempted to interpret it somewhat differently. Mahadev Desai (1956) used this translation for his research on the Gita according to Gandhi, a version of which received Gandhi's approval. Desai maintained that Gandhi's translation reinterpreted the Gita as emphasizing the equality of all human beings before God, as professing the dynamic evolutionary nature of the Indian society, and as holding the belief that man is an active creature struggling for a better life both as an individual and as part of a collective. Thus, almost in the same way that Greek philosophy was interpreted during the Enlightenment (Gay, 1967), ancient Indian philosophy was reinterpreted as an antecedent of modern philosophy.

This redefinition and utilization of traditional values and their institutional transformation in modern terms was a major strategy adopted by educated elites to integrate the country as well as to maintain their position. Thus, we see that the erosion of traditional institutions in India was accompanied by the formation of new patterns of legitimation and integration.

MODERN APPROACHES TO INTEGRATION

The modern Indian approach to integration, gradually developed from the beginning of the nineteenth century, has been based on a rational, realistic appraisal of India's situation. Essentially, the modern Indian approach accepts diversity as a given. It assumes, first of all, that Indian society is composed of different but equal social units, and second, that these units freely compete and cooperate with one another and so adjust their expectations, creating a national identity (*Report of the Commission on Emotional Integration,* 1962:3). Finally, the units are considered capable of controlling or mitigating internal conflicts. In this way, social integration in India has become a practical problem of "determining how far the free play of provincial sentiment deriving from consciousness of cultural and linguistic distinctiveness is a factor in creating unity or disunity" (Bondurant, 1958:49).

In order to realize this pattern of integration, four principles were formulated in operative terms: (1) gradual "harmonious" change; (2) mechanical solidarity; (3) unity in diversity; and (4) discriminative egalitarianism.[3]

Gradual Harmonious Change

The notion of gradual socio-economic change is the most critical to the understanding of the Indian concept of integration. It is based on the assumption that Indian unity largely depends on the pattern and rhythm of change. Peaceful, gradual, and harmonious transformation is perceived as a necessary precondition for social integration.

This approach can easily be interpreted as serving the interests of the ruling classes; in fact, it is based on the notion that the central elites are essential to unity and that in order to ensure their commitment to this task their privileges have to be maintained. Gradual change contributes to the reinforcement of the elites' position in two ways: it helps to slow down their decline and to postpone the full redistribution of wealth until the gross national product is significantly increased. This "stable" principle of gradual transition, however, is accompanied by almost free political interplay among various groups which both promotes change and assures, to a certain extent, the correlation between wealth, power, and political dominancy.

In accordance with this approach, the Indian mainstream regards economic development as a goal to be achieved through persuasion and slow, balanced change. Any rapid economic development is viewed as potentially dangerous: "For such a program to be quickly successful it may be necessary to give up personal freedom of action and to accept the destruction of ancient customs and ways of life, and to adopt totalitarianism" (*Report of the University Education Commission, 1948/49*, p. 196).

Even the critical issue of food supply assumes less important in the light of those values that are components of integration.

> India has also other needs than food. The new India has committed herself to the upholding of human freedom, to the recognition of individual worth, and to the nurture of human dignity and self respect. The food problem of India must be solved by means which are... the foundation stones on which the structure of the new Indian society is being built (*Report of the University Education Commission, 1948/49*, p. 196).

This approach (which was not developed randomly) is based on the assumption that any divergence between economic and other goals will endanger social integration. Any discord is a threat to the whole and should be decreased, though not necessarily eliminated. Potential conflict can be reduced by avoiding radical institutional changes which may upset the given balance between different primordial groups and endanger integration.

Economic development as a goal in itself is a victim of this approach. Although rapid economic change can be considered an integrative factor since it can raise standards of living and thereby diminish discontent, it can also be considered disintegrative inasmuch as it may contribute to the erosion of traditional control while not necessarily providing adequate institutions for conflict resolution.

Since the beginning of the century Indian elites have had to strike a balance between the rhythm of economic change (with the concomitant rise of new social aspirations and the diminishing effectiveness of old mechanisms of social control) and integration. Increased literacy, educational opportunities, and the mass media have led to less tolerance of gradual economic change. Thus, the question of whether to encourage rapid change, thereby weakening social control, or to promote gradual change, with the accompanying danger of famine and mass protest, has become a real social problem. The Indian elites have attempted to reach a compromise between developmental and integrative aims by minimizing structural change as well as by curbing the emergence of free-floating manpower. It seems that the Indian elites have tended to balance economic change with the maintenance of traditional mechanisms of control (Shah, 1967:7ff). Certain issues, however, will eventually have to be faced, such as how long integration and starvation can coexist and at what level of subsistence integrative mechanisms will cease to operate.

"Mechanical" Solidarity

The "mechanical" element (in Durkheim's sense) in the Indian definition of integration is represented by the concept of emotional integration (T.N. Sheth, 1960). The concept contains ethical, symbolic, and sentimental aspects and was created by Indian elites as a conscious attempt to legitimate their position and to strengthen Indian solidarity (AICE, 1967:60ff).

Early in the 1920s the concept was labelled "patriotism" and defined in terms of Western romantic historicism. In Lajpat Rai's words:

> Patriotism, however, does not include only the material and the physical aspects of a country. It includes all that Renan has called *L'ame d'une nation,* the more delicate shadings of feelings, such as piety for the past, admiration and love of the heroic figures in the history of the nation, and its great achievements; love of language, community of tradition, law and customs, and all that gives individual character to the civilization of each nation (1920:37).

Lajpat Rai's concepts were developed by Professor H. Kabir in the *Report of the Seminar on National Integration* (1958). Kabir defined Indian unity as a "common Indian consciousness" which harmonized individuality and collectivity among different groups and sectors on a structural and emotional basis.

In a later seminar (1962) it was assumed that while political integration had received appropriate attention, emotional aspects had been neglected. The basic goal underlying emotional integration was defined as developing an "organic" social entity rather than an "amorphous mass.... Nationhood has a strong psychological basis and depends on the people concerned having had similar experiences... and interpreting them in the same way" (*Report of the Commission on Emotional Integration,* 1962:1). Patriotism in India did not develop "merely as a result of the presence of a common enemy" (the British), but "because there has always been a sense of belonging to, and identification with, this India and a sense of pride in, and affection for it" (*Report of the Commission on Emotional Integration,* 1962:4). The commission further indicated that this emotional identification was based not only on religion but on geographic symbols as well. The conclusion was that the notion of emotional integration derived from the metaphysical assumption of the unity of the universe and the transcendental similarity of all its creatures (*Report of the Commission on Emotional Integration,* 1962:5–7). The vagueness of this definition facilitated its acceptance by most parts of the population.

In reality, however, the notion of emotional integration has been relatively inapplicable in the context of the Indian primordial diversity. Unity is constitutional and intellectual, whereas diversity is emotional, linguistic, and ethnic. In such circumstances, diversity is surely the strongest sentiment. Nevertheless, the Indian concept of emotional integration, referring to a cluster of traditional symbols interpreted in modern terms of nationhood and ethics, has been used to legitimize Indian unity as well as to enhance the positions of the Indian educated class.

Unity in Diversity

One of the fundamental elements of integration is expressed by the slogan "unity in diversity." The Indian people are conceived as being "welded into one, and made into one strong national unity maintaining at the same time all [their] wonderful diversity."[4] This umbrella concept combines most definitions of social integration and is based on an awareness of the dangers of pursuing a monolithic approach (*Report of the Seminar on National Integration,* 1958:13,30;*Seminar,* 1969:115).

The definition of "unity in diversity" stems from the assumption that "unity is not uniformity" nor is it "colorless – sameness in all respects" (*Report of the Commission on Emotional Integration,* 1962:2). Fundamentally, unity is perceived in cultural terms. "When I think of an Indian unity," said Nehru, "...the long vista of India's history stretches before me, not so much the succession of kings and emperors, but rather that of the inner life of a nation, its cultural activities in many fields, its spiritual adventures and its voyages in the realm of thought and action" (1949:11).

The concept is not based on the definition of pluralism as applied to modern society since it refers to a primordial division of labor and not to cross-cutting affiliations. The concept denotes the cooperation of different cultures and total membership groups considered equal under the aegis of one government. In other words, India is a cultural and political federation of different primordial groups (Panikkar, 1963:227).

The principle of unity in diversity can be demonstrated in the constitutional provisions that recognize the existence of different primordial groups.

For example, Article 29 declares that "any section of the citizens residing in the territory of India or any part thereof having a distinct language, script or culture of its own shall have the right to conserve the same." More important, this provision has been institutionalized by the creation of a special office, the Commissioner for Linguistic Minorities (J. Das Gupta, 1970).

The underlying assumption of this concept is that Indian diversity is the basis of its strength. In the words of Pankikkar, that all regions "should feel proud of their tradition and history as parts of India and should emphasize their special contributions to India's culture is not a source of weakness but of national strength" (1963:226). Although some of these regional-cultural groups evoke particularistic images, they do not threaten the concept of a united India since,

> ...if the Bengalis feel that they have made a unique contribution to the growth of the national idea in India,... the Marathas feel that they are an imperial people, and the Punjabis that they are the swordarm of India, these are aspects of a self-image that people have created, which do not interfere with a nation's development (Panikkar, 1963:226).

The Indian definition of unity in diversity implies integration in terms of the very forces which could eventually work against it — that is, in terms of separate collective identities which may lead to disintegration. "Communalism" is a term used in India to denote the processes by which primordial affiliation, usually combined with a political organization, causes "tension between different sections of the people" (*Report of the National Integration Council and Unit, Summary Record,* 1969:3). Once politicized, such affiliations as religious organization, casteism, and regionalism exemplify communalism. India's problem has not been how to reduce disintegrative forces but rather how to utilize communalistic factors to bring about integration.

R. Kothari explains that it is through the political articulation of particularistic identities that a more stable pattern of integration becomes possible, and that it is in cases where such an open articulation has not been permitted that the outcome tends to be anomic and lacking efficacious behavior. On the other hand, we have also seen that such articulation leads to a gradual but definite shift in organizational and symbolic affiliations, gives rise to structures that mediate between society and polity, and with time creates a cultural mix that provides an anchor to the modernist political center (Kothari, 1970a:247–248).

National identity in India has been defined as a corporation of particularistic forces. The paradox can be explained dialectically. Firstly, primordial groups express their separate identities through reconstruction and glorification of their past and through organization into distinct political and cultural entities. Secondly, their identities strengthened, they develop symmetrical (cultural and political) relationships with other groups in the society and with the center. On the strength of these relationships, they maintain that they are not parasitical on Indian culture, but rather contribute to it as equals. Thus, social integration can be achieved more easily when groups have some kind of contact, even if it leads to conflict, than when they remain totally isolated from one another. It appears that conflict of some sort is a necessary stage in building an integrated society.

Finally, each group is defined in terms of its relationship to the whole. The product is a primordial interdependence or "organic" solidarity (Bondurant, 1958:49–50).

Discriminative Egalitarianism

The "organic" definition of integration is buttressed by the concept of equality: each primordial group, according to its relative size, has the formal right to be treated in the same manner as every other group. The concept of equality embraces all aspects of Indian life, including cultural and political representation and economic cooperation (Husain, 1961:212ff). Equal treatment does not affect communal affiliations and given hierarchies but rather incorporates them into the system.

Srinivas, participating in the Seminar on National Integration, described the hierarchical nature of egalitarianism in India:

> It would be cynical to doubt the existence of these egalitarian forces. But one point about them needs to be mentioned: each layer in Indian society wants to be the equal of the layers above it but refuses to concede equality to the layers below it. Thus, the "middle" castes want to be regarded as the equals of Brahmins, though they themselves are not willing to concede that the "low" castes are as good as themselves. The Harijans want to assert that they are the equals of everyone. The point to note here is that what is usually stated to be the demand for equality is nothing more than group-mobility. Every group wants to rise to the top and it wants to dissociate itself with groups which are considered inferior *(Report of the Seminar on National Integration,* 1958:24).

The concept of discriminative egalitarianism is particularly evident in the case of backward classes. The Constitution of India lays down certain safeguards for scheduled castes and tribes as well as backward classes, which are the weakest segments of the population. These safeguards provide for a prescribed number of seats in the legislature, recruitment of tribal candidates to posts in the Union and state governments, and the creation of administrative instruments for dealing with their problems (Tape, 1967). Welfare allocations and other benefits, such as scholarship grants, legal aid, and even investments, have often been partially determined on a primordial basis, that is, on the basis of caste and linguistic diversity.[5]

This preferential treatment in allocating national resources provides, at the very least, a formal legitimation for particularistic economic and political demands of different groups; thus it partially prevents the market mechanism from being used as a regulative principle against these groups.

The use of pure laissez faire principles in an open-market system is naturally beneficial for members of the upper strata. Their initial advantageous position and ability to utilize it in an open market widens the gap between themselves and the lower strata and increases polarization. The image of protective discrimination and the principles accompanying it cannot be perceived as merely an attempt to compensate the weaker strata or to increase equality, but rather as a conscious effort to legitimize primordial affiliations and to embody them into the system. The fact that the criteria for such preferential politics are often based on universal criteria (e.g., level of income and literacy rate) is important. The image contains a universalistic definition of particularistic privileges and complements the concept of unity in diversity, both of which are based on the assumption that by increasing splits integration is also enhanced.

These four principles constitute the Indian approach to integration. The first two generally serve the interests of the major elites, while the latter two, those of the peripheral groups. In this way, some balance is achieved between the interests of the center and the periphery.

CONCLUSIONS

As the traditional Indian pattern of legitimacy and integration declined, new concepts were developed. The basic feature of the reconstructed concepts was that they synthesized antagonistic criteria, such as particularistic and universalistic or "mechanic" and "organic" ones, and combined customary patterns with modern concepts of integration. Our discussion leads us to raise a number of questions: How did the elites translate these antagonistic concepts into institutions? Why were they interested in doing so? How have antagonistic principles and arrangements been bridged? These issues will be discussed in later chapters.

NOTES

1. "The general trend of the Gita is, in my opinion, unmistakable. It is accepted by all Hindu sects as authoritative. It is free from any form of dogma. In short compass it gives a complete, reasoned, moral code. It satisfies both the intellect and the heart. It is thus both philosophical and devotional. Its appeal is universal" (Gandhi, 1965:80).

2. "There is no wisdom for a man without harmony, and without harmony there is no contemplation. Without contemplation there cannot be peace, and without peace there cannot be joy" (Bhagavadgita, 1962: Ch.IX).

3. Methodologically, we have used four types of sources for the analysis of the modern Indian concept of integration. These are: (1) writings of recognized leaders; (2) official declarations; (3) reports of official committees on national integration; and (4) scholarly works.

4. This statement, from a speech made by Nehru in Bangalore in October 1955, has often been quoted by national leaders.

5. On the legislative and political consequences of the image of protective discrimination, see Galanter, 1979, and our later discussion.

Chapter 5

INDIAN DUAL ELITES AND THEIR PATTERNS OF LEGITIMATION

INTRODUCTION

The utilization of traditional concepts of integration in the formulation of modern ones could not have been accomplished without the presence of educated elites to serve as mediators between different value premises and segments of society.[1] To understand this process, it is necessary to examine the basic characteristics of these elites and manner in which they emerged and utilized their resources. The central thesis of this chapter is that the Indian educated[2] formed a dually oriented elite combining modern and traditional identities and that it was this duality which enabled them to selectively reconstruct tradition and convert it into national symbols.

Educated Indians have often been described as dual persons who appear to be both within and between East and West or traditional and modernity (Chaudhuri, 1951; McCully, 1966; Shils, 1961, 1966; Srinivas, 1969; Stonequist, 1964; Tangri, 1960).

Three patterns of duality can be distinguished: the conflict-ridden, the differentiated, and the hybrid. In the first, the individual is involved in two or more cultures and cannot decide which is preferable. In the differentiated pattern the behavioral code adhered to depends upon the varying demands of institutional settings. For example, the individual may behave according to one code in familial (traditional) situations and another when filling administrative (more modern) roles. Finally, in the hybrid type two or more very different or contradictory codes of behavior are merged. While in private life the conflict-ridden and differentiated types have been common, on the national level the hybrid type has dominated.

Various biographies and autobiographies (e.g., Chaudhuri, 1951; Karve, 1963; Tandon, 1968), Indian interpretations of traditional sources (e.g., Tilak, 1935; Gandhi, 1968), and British descriptions of the Indian educated (e.g., McCully, 1966:390–391; *Report of the Calcutta University Commission*, 1919: I,I/122–128) all support this premise. Even official Indian sources have commented on the combination of India's two "souls": "Two contradictory impulses have attracted Indian intellectuals. One is a jealous pride in Indian genius and tradition wholly distinct from those of the West. The other is the no less jealous desire to profit by the example of the West" (*Report of the University Education Commission, 1948/49*, p. 56).

Perhaps the clearest description of the hybrid pattern of duality among the educated was given by Nehru:

> I have become a queer mixture of the East and the West, out of place everywhere, at home nowhere. Perhaps my thoughts and approach to life are more akin to what is called Western than Eastern, but India clings to me, as she does to all her children, in innumerable ways; and behind me lie, somewhere in the subconscious, racial memories of a hundred, or whatever the number may be, generations of Brahmans. I cannot get rid of either that past inheritance or my recent acquisition. They are both part of me, and though they help me in both the East and the West, they also create in me a feeling of spiritual loneliness not only in public activities but in life itself. I am a stranger and alien in the West. I cannot be of it. But in my own country also, sometimes, I have an exile's feeling (1941, quoted in Smith, 1958).

The remainder of this chapter explores the basis for the hybridism of Indian educated elites and then demonstrates how that duality was articulated so as to create national symbols and institutions.

THE EMERGENCE OF A HYBRID ELITE

How is it that Indian elites emerged from the modern educational system, particularly the universities, as hybrid types? The answer may be partially found in the nature of modern education in India.[3] Initially the British developed the educational system in India largely in response to their need to solve the "basic paradox" faced by most colonial powers: how to maximize profits without endangering established modes of legitimation and integration. The British found the most efficient solution to be the creation of middlemen able to link traditional and modern structures.[4]

Three phases can be discerned in the British educational policy.[5] Firstly, traditional learning was encouraged, although a few elitist schools in the English tradition were established to ensure a supply of local manpower for assistance in government administration. In the second phase, beginning in 1835, the declared objective was the promotion of Western culture by means of the English language in the hope that a mediatory group of upper-class Indians could be trained. But when these modern educated Indians began to interpret their traditions according to modern concepts and use them against the British, the latter felt a need to institute another change in educational policy. The shift was to a combination of modern and vernacular learning in an attempt to mitigate the rise of radical ideas and to create mediators familiar with both traditional and modern cultures. In this Anglo-vernacular stage the university system was established (1854) and active measures were taken to extend educational opportunities to all classes by using their respective languages. Students were expected to be bilingual and bicultural and able to synthesize Western and Indian values. Consequently, the universities rapidly became nurseries for dual persons identifying with both cultures rather than with neither.

It is important to note that a large proportion of the educated elites originated in the higher castes, particularly the Brahmins.[6] Exposure to the English pattern of education, with its emphasis on the humanities and, consequently, non-manual occupations, provided the Brahmins as a *varna* with opportunities to maintain and reinforce their traditional status.

The "Brahminization" of Western education was important in two respects. First, the large number of Brahmins who entered the modern education system motivated members of other castes to aspire to do so as well, thus making secondary and higher education a popular channel for mobility. Consequently, the number of non-Brahmins receiving education gradually increased (and the proportion of Brahmins decreased accordingly). This process began to accelerate in the early 1940s, so that almost every caste eventually became represented in the educated elite. This ultimately increased the connection between center and periphery.

Second, the penetration of Brahmins into Western higher education gave an aura of traditional prestige to modern elites and was an ipso facto legitimation of the modern educational system. By the later stages of the colonial period educational and political representation of castes became more equal, a fact which indirectly contributed to the pluralistic nature of the Indian regime. The gradual process of modernization undergone by the Brahmins permitted the maintenance of some traditional patterns of legitimacy in Indian society, while at the same time it encouraged the development of "a new base of resources free from commitments to the traditional arrangements" (Heesterman, 1973:103). On the whole, Indian elites have used their duality to integrate society (Brecher, 1971). How and why Indian elites have done so may be illustrated by the pattern in which they created a collective national identity.

THE FORMATION OF NATIONAL SYMBOLS

The emergence of Indian nationalism can be viewed as a value-added process, developing from a cultural-symbolic phase into an institutional one and from an elitist movement into a more popular-oriented one.[7]

Between the end of the eighteenth and the middle of the nineteenth centuries the first wave of Indian educated elites created what has been called the Hindu Renaissance (promoted by Raja Rammohun Roy and various cultural societies, such as the Brahma Samaj movement and early versions of the Arya Samaj). The Renaissance essentially constituted a rational attempt to reconstruct some parts of Indian tradition in modern terms and to delicately balance Indian and Western cultures. Although the approach at this stage was eclectic, a conscious effort was made to convert cultural symbols into political-oriented associations, the more important among these being the Indian League and the Indian National Conference.

A new phase began in the early 1900s with an extension of earlier attempts to construct a hybrid culture (McLane, 1977). This crucial process of reconstruction of tradition merits an in-depth examination since it illustrates how the newly emerged elites institutionalized their own cultural dilemma. "Reconstruction" is defined here as a process in which some parts of past tradition are innovatively reinterpreted on the symbolic level and converted into institutions in order to legitimize new concepts of social order. Four strategies used by Indian intellectuals for legitimizing cultural change can be identified (Kahane, 1975); of these, three are primarily expressive and one is mainly instrumental but with significant expressive undertones.

Similarization involves the reinterpretation of the traditions or history of one culture so that it becomes almost identical with that of another. Indian intellectuals reconstructed parts of their past in a manner that enabled them to claim that many modern values and institutions and much scientific knowledge were of Indian origin or at least attributable to the Aryans, who provided a common ancestry for Europe and India. The adoption of modern values was regarded as merely a revival of India's own ancient values. Continuity was thereby established between past and present, and the foreign flavor of new values was minimized.

Through a process of *universalization,* the Indians stripped their traditional values and knowledge of their particularistic origins and gave them a more universal meaning. In this way, the absorption of new ideas was not perceived as imitating some particular culture but merely as relating Indian culture to general human values.

Symmetrization relates to legitimizing the adoption of new values through a definition of the process as a mutual or balanced exchange between cultures. Based on the principle that it is legitimate to adopt the values of another culture if the borrower can repay in kind, it complements similarization and universalization. Past Indian contributions to the existing body of knowledge were cited in this respect, as were certain values, such as nonviolence, anti-materialism, and cooperation, described as Indian in origin. The underlying assumption was that superior experience and virtue in specific humanistic areas justified India's approaching the West as an equal. The most important aspect of symmetrization was its contribution to the legitimization of those values that were not considered part of Indian culture. Just as the Indians would not wish their contributions to the West rejected, they should not reject Western science and philosophy "because the discoverers of these sciences happen to be non-Indians..." (Lajpat Rai, 1920:76). Symmetrization enabled the Indians to view the process of adoption as one of balanced, reciprocal exchange.

Finally, a *functional* approach was utilized, based on justifying the adoption of Western ideas in terms of social needs and national survival. This method constitutes a more pragmatic or instrumental approach since it was assumed that new developments in economics, science, and technology were as essential for India as for any other developing country. But even in this attempt at functional justification, the emphasis was on expressive as well as instrumental elements. The adoption of Western concepts was described in terms of their contribution to national independence and pride and to international recognition.

In summary, the various strategies adopted by the Indian intellectuals in interpreting their tradition allowed them to adopt new values while maintaining some degree of cultural continuity. In this way, they built the cultural foundation for legitimizing a new type of regime. This process of cultural reconstruction continued throughout the period under research. However, from the twenties attempts were made to translate the symbols into action and institutions. This brings us to the next phase in the growth of the Indian national movement.

From the 1920s, after Gandhi assumed the national leadership, political organizations which had been established became more populist-oriented and directed at the periphery. To some extent, these developments were also the result of British constitutional reforms (1919–1920), which made the Indian political system more flexible and representative (Bhagwan, 1974). It was at this stage that a national ideology and institutions became crystallized and the Indian political elite assumed a more popular image, attracting peripheral support. The popularization of the national movement was possible because of a large group of educated Indians emerging from the universities and capable of fusing the elements of Indian society.

As J.M. Brown (1972:356) rightly emphasizes, Gandhi's success in broadening the base of Indian politics during this phase cannot be explained solely by his charismatic appeal. Rather, it was chiefly due to his ability to utilize middlemen, for the most part the educated, who originated in all parts of the periphery and wielded influence there.

> The precondition of support for [the] non-cooperation [movement] from those outside the ranks of the political nation was the involvement of intermediate layers of leadership beneath the politicians who responded to Gandhi's appeal and were both willing and able to organize their localities or their personal following in support of his campaign (J.M. Brown, 1972:318).

The diffusion of educated mediators in almost every province and district was an attempt to involve the whole of Indian society in his political movement.

> [Gandhi] made contact with groups of subcontractors who found in the techniques he offered ways of defending or promoting their local interests. The result was no monolithic political movement. Instead,

non-cooperation became a chameleon campaign, taking colour from its surroundings as it was shaped in each locality by the particular forces at work and the strains and stresses of the local power structure (J.M. Brown, 1972:322).

Gandhi's appeal, then, was based on his capacity to give old meaning to new concepts and new meaning to the old and to translate them into institutions. The non-cooperation movement was the test of his political methods for mobilizing wider support. Although his methods frequently encouraged local sentiments and clashes of interests, on the whole, they succeeded in providing a popular base for Indian nationalism (J.M. Brown, 1972:322–323). As the national movement became more popular, the gap between center and periphery was reduced and the relationship between them was institutionalized.

At this point it would seem appropriate to consider the reasons why the educated elites have been interested in reducing the gap and institutionalizing a rather close relationship with the periphery. Since the 1920s the Indian educational system has produced large numbers of graduates, many of whom have hardly been able to find adequate employment, if at all.[8] Unemployed or underemployed educated who have not been part of the establishment have provided India with a counter-elite which has turned to the periphery for support. As this counter-elite has grown, it has come to threaten established elites. The result has been the institutionalization of a more populist and competitive political culture.

CONCLUSIONS

Hybrid elites emerged out of the Indian university system and utilized their duality in the construction of national symbols combining contradictory elements. These symbols were then used to legitimize a populist national movement, integrating societal groups into a unified framework which resembled a sovereign state within the British colonial system. Furthermore, their hybrid nature also enabled the elites to operate unique intermediary institutions to cope with conflicting elements in the society. The nature of these institutions is the subject of the next two chapters.

NOTES

1. There are three major approaches to the mediatory power of the educated in the sociological tradition. The first maintains that the educated as a group possess "objective" knowledge above pure interests. Consequently, they can serve a mediatory function as a third party (Mannheim, 1940:16–47). The second approach claims that professionals tend to be more objective, universalistic, and collective-oriented, not because they belong to a disinterested or "altruistic"-oriented group, but because such behavior best serves their interests (Parsons, 1964:34–49). While this approach takes into account both the interests and institutional position of the educated, it hardly explains why they operate as a mediatory power. Lastly, the educated have been perceived as having greater freedom to manipulate their interests than most other groups due to their resources.

Hence, their institutional position allows them to act as middlemen between various groups and principles (Coser, 1970; Parkin, 1968:191). In fact, no a priori premises can be made about the behavior of the educated without considering the conditions under which they function. In other words, one has to specify the social conditions under which the educated may assume a mediatory role.

2. The term "educated" is used here as a general concept, embracing those of "intelligentsia," "intellectuals" and "professionals," and defined as a group of people who possess and use different kinds of knowledge usually acquired at a university or its equivalent.

3. Details will be provided in my monograph, *Higher Education and Elite Formation in India* (forthcoming).

4. In most developing societies modern elites have largely emerged from the universities (Foster, 1965; Lipset and Solari, 1967). Modern educational channels have often been used by colonial powers to produce middlemen able to link them with the traditional masses. However, the result has often been the production of economic brokers rather than cultural mediators.

5. The analysis is based on information from Cunningham, 1968; McCully, 1966.

6. Three categories of *jatis* surpassed the Brahmins in terms of educational achievements. These were relatively small homogeneous groups and included those *jatis* that were perceived and acted as almost one group together with the Brahmins (as the Baidya together with the Brahmins constituted the Bhardlok in Bengal); the relatively rich *jatis* of landlords or merchants (such as the Baidya in Bengal, the Lohana in Bombay, and the Baniya in the Central Provinces, Punjab, and the United Provinces); and the *jatis* of writers who considered education important to their profession (such as the Kayastha in Bihar and the United Provinces). For data on these *jatis*, see the *Census of India, 1931*, Vol. I, Pt. II, Table XIV, pp. 450–470. For more details, see Bhattacharya, 1896:151–152, 175, 198–199, 211ff, 217, 234–235; Broomfield, 1968; Ghurye, 1969; Kahane, 1981.

7. The analysis is abstracted from the works of D'Cruz, 1967; A.R. Desai, 1954; Ghose, 1959; Kopf, 1974; Majumdar et al., 1963; Malik, 1977; McLane, 1977; Misra, 1976; Radhakrishnan, 1974; Lajpat Rai, 1966, 1967; Rothermund, 1979; R.R. Roy, 1906, 1962; Seal, 1968.

8. Between 1911/12 and 1930/31 the number of students in higher education rose by 155 percent, while the number of public administration posts increased by only 2 percent. Similarly, over the period 1960/61–1970/71 the number of students grew by 191 percent, whereas the number of administrative posts rose by only 50 percent. See *Statistical Abstract for British India, 1911/12–1920/21*, Table 151, p. 299; *Statistical Abstract for British India, 1930/31*, Table 137, p. 299; *University Grants Commission: Report for the Year 1970/71*, Appendix X-III, p. 43.

Chapter 6

BRIDGING MECHANISMS:
INTERMEDIARY POLITICAL INSTITUTIONS

INTRODUCTION

In preceding chapters we analyzed Indian elites in terms of their ability to develop cultural and institutional frameworks and to mediate between structural contradictions. What has not yet been discussed are the tools they have utilized to institutionalize antagonism.

Due to the inability to resolve contradictions in the Indian context, four means of coping with antagonism were open to elites: differentiation, mixture, compromise, and fusion (see Ch. 1). Of these options, only the last one enabled them to ensure both social change and stability. This, however, required the use of mediatory bridging mechanisms. As we stated in Chapter 1, bridging mechanisms are characterized by exhaustiveness, structural complexity, institutional ambiguousness, an open structure, and symmetry.

As the overall characteristics of Indian politics have already undergone extensive research (e.g., Brass, 1974, Kothari, 1970a), our discussion will merely focus upon the system's mediatory traits.

Mediatory mechanisms can be said to operate in five spheres: between behavioral codes, institutional arrangements, and group or individual interests; and within and between central and peripheral entities. Often the same mediatory mechanisms operate in many spheres and on many levels.

Mediatory institutions (or mechanisms) can be classified according to their internal structure. In that sense, one may distinguish three major types: (1) those that are almost fully open to bargaining and are organized as corporate bodies (political mechanisms); (2) those that are based on "objective" principles and therefore are relatively closed to bargaining ("objective" mechanisms); and (3) those mechanisms that are mixed, that is, contain both open and closed patterns.

The difference between political and non-political "objective" mechanisms is related to both the extent to which the rules of the game are negotiable and the pattern in which these rules are articulated. Along these lines, seven mediatory institutions may be distinguished in India. Three of them belong to the first type. These are the political parties, factional and caste associations, and federal arrangements. Three others refer mostly to the last type (mixed), although they place more weight upon "objective" principles. These include the legal system, *panchayat* (municipal) institutions, and Indian civil service (state and national bureaucracies), all of which operate according to a combination of statutory and negotiable principles. A seventh mediatory mechanism, the mass media (and especially the press), will also be briefly explored with regard to its use as an instrument of communication among elites. The discussion of "objective" mechanisms will be left to the following chapter, while the present one will deal with political mechanisms. The latter will basically be defined as institutional arrangements in which the haggling over terms is highly legitimized and based on the existing power structure and interests.

We have mentioned three political bridging mechanisms. The spatial relationship among them can be described as follows: the political party system provides a framework for a power struggle on both the state and the national levels, the factional system provides the means for intra-party struggles, and the federal arrangement provides an arena for the institutionalization of inter-primordial (state) conflicts.

It should be noted that the parliament (*Lok Sabha*) can be regarded as an instrument for negotiation but not as a mediatory mechanism because it is not directly linked to any specific population group or societal sector.

THE INDIAN POLITICAL PARTIES

Introduction

Two broad structural types of political parties are commonly distinguished: the roof and skeleton types.[1] The roof type of political party is defined as a market-like organization composed of different groups (rather than individuals) whose common denominator, beyond ad hoc situational alliance, is vague; in that sense, it is a pluralistic or umbrella party. The skeleton type is nearly the opposite — a centralized organization based on a homogeneous, stable and cohesive membership (Duverger, 1954). The difference between the two types may be perceived as the extent to which loyalty to, or membership in, the party — or within the groups comprising the party — is fluid.

The concept "political fluidity" refers here to the degree to which manpower can be mobilized for political action (e.g., protests, strikes, and voting support). Fluidity usually depends on the scope and intensity of ties and obligations within groups. The weaker the ties and the greater the differentiation in affiliation, the greater the fluidity of manpower.[2]

Political fluidity in India is unique inasmuch as it is based on non-differentiated patterns of social affiliation and relationships. Most parties are regarded as fluid corporations of various non-fluid groups. On the intra-party level the entire system is fluid in the sense that almost any coalition or alignment is possible.[3]

The Indian party system is very diverse. The "same" political party may differ in name, nature, and membership from area to area and sometimes even from election to election within one particular area. What remains relatively stable is that most are built as corporations based on an ad hoc, tentative, conditional merger of various groups. It is this trait which largely contributes to the intermediary power of Indian political parties.

The mediatory characteristics of the parties will be analyzed on two levels: the party system as a whole and the major blocs within it.

The Indian Party System

Following Schumpeter (1950), the Indian party system can be defined as an institutional arrangement in which potential leaders affiliated with particular groups attempt to acquire power and make political decisions through a competitive struggle for popular support. Most of the parties are aggregations of primordial and/or interest groups which are particularistic in nature and cooperate with one another for varying lengths of time. This cooperation is largely ad hoc and conditioned by the possible benefits to be gained. Therefore, each party, as well as the entire system, operates in a market-like structure in which various leaders negotiate with one another for the greatest available benefits, using votes as currency. Loyalty or commitment based on broad universal and stable criteria is limited. The Indian political market is somewhat like a pyramid. At the base are many "small" group leaders (of various independent groups) who operate as petty merchants or peddlers; in the middle are leaders who operate as retail merchants; and at the top are a few "big" leaders — the largest corporations, such as the Congress and Janata parties — who act as wholesale merchants. The wholesalers buy small leaders and possess some power to dictate prices in the political market.

In recent years the Indian party system has undergone some changes regarding its relative strength and social composition (see Ch. 8). However, despite these changes, or perhaps because of them, it has more or less retained the corporate structure (Brass, 1977; Eldersveld and Bashiruddin, 1978).

On the national level the party system consisted of three major blocs (at least until the 1977 elections): the left-wing Communist parties the right-wing Hindu parties (mainly Jan Sangh and Swatantra); and the core of the system, the Congress Party, which is composed of various sub-groups and factions covering the entire spectrum of Indian politics.[4] Since independence there have been several splits and mergers within the parties, but the basic characteristics of the system seem to have remained the same. A poll of valid voters which covers the national elections up to 1977 indicates that the Congress Party has always attracted about 35–45 percent of the votes, whereas the right wing has had the support of 10–17 percent, and the left, about 10 percent. The remaining votes have been divided among small parties and independent candidates (see Table 6:1).

Legitimation and Integration in India

TABLE 6:1

THE LOK SABHA: DISTRIBUTION OF VALID VOTES BY PARTY

	1952	1957	1962	1967	1971	1977
Congress	44.99%	47.78%	44.72%	40.73%	43.64%*	35.54%*
					10.36**	
Swatantra	–	–	7.89	8.68	3.08	
Jan Sangh	3.06	5.93	6.44	9.41	7.48	43.17***
SSP	16.00	–	2.69	4.92	2.43	
CPI	3.29	8.92	9.94	5.19	4.89	2.82
CPI (M)	–	–	–	4.21	4.97	4.30
PSP	–	10.41	6.81	3.06	0.98	–
Others	16.00	–	10.63	10.10	13.54	9.15
Independents	16.00	26.96	11.08	13.75	8.33	6.02

Sources: For the years 1952–1971: R.L. Gupta, 1972, Table 2.
For 1977: *The Overseas Hindustan Times,* April 21, 1977.

* New   ** Old   *** Janata Party

Essentially, the distribution of voters and membership among parties only partially impinges on class and socio-economic standing (Kothari, 1970a: 211–212). Dasgupta and Morris-Jones (1976) discovered some differences in the socio-economic makeup of the various parties, but these seem to be too small to be significant in such a divisive society. However, on the institutional level, each party manifestly represents specific interests. Lower class interests are more likely to be represented in left-wing parties (especially the Communists), while more capitalistic interests are represented in the right bloc and center.

The Indian political pyramid can be described as highly diversified on the local level, while showing more centripetal tendencies on the state and national levels. The centrifugal tendencies on the local level enlarge the representation and bargaining power of small groups. This may be an indication of the system's weakness, since splits and the free manipulation of small particularistic powers often impede the development of rational policies.

On the local level each party is centered around a few, usually educated, lesser leaders who are able to manipulate the interaction between the traditional structure and the modern competitive system (Morris–Jones, 1976). Their power base is usually connected with one particular *jati* or area. Considered members of the *jati*, they are bound by its rules and obligations, and their major role is defined as the translation of primordial affiliations into political power. So long as results are beneficial, their freedom to operate is fairly wide. The whole party system can thus be seen as a composition of small groups that manipulate their power on the local level and compete to sell it on the state or national level (Carter, 1974; see also the discussion on caste associations in this chapter).

When inter-group competition increases substantially on the local level, the mobilizers of power become "political peddlers" and, as a result, "pure" market principles are eventually abandoned. Naturally, the emergence of a political market of peddlers increases conflict. Thus, while serving as an arena for interest representation and institutionalization of social conflicts, the party system also accentuates clashes, although it eventually copes with them. This process can be clarified by an analysis of the major blocs in the Indian party system.

The Major Political Blocs

The mediatory role of the Indian parties may largely be explained by their patterns of manpower mobilization and by the way in which interests are manipulated, rather than by the degree to which they are represented. In that sense, the parties can be analytically divided into five major blocs: (1) the national corporate parties, which mobilize multiple interests in an institutionalized way (the Congress or Janata parties); (2) parties which institutionally mobilized and articulate primordial sentiments on the national level (e.g., the Jan Sangh and the Muslim League); (3) parties which institutionally mobilize and operate socio-economic or class interests (e.g., the Swatantra for the middle class and the Communist parties for the lower classes); (4) parties which institutionally mobilize local, particularistic affiliations and connect them to the center (e.g., the DMK and Akali Dal); and (5) ad hoc parties or movements which generally mobilize sentiments and/or interests through semi- or extra-institutional means in order to promote the goals of their members (this category ranges from "Independent" candidates to the Naxalite movement).

1. *The national corporate party: the Congress Party.* The Congress Party, in its various political manifestations, represents the most centripetal body in the Indian party system in that it is composed of various large shareholders and peddlers of the political market. This framework was gradually constructed, beginning in 1885, when the Indian National Congress Party was founded as a narrowly based association promoting the interests of landlords and the educated middle class. The party began by agitating for a greater degree of national autonomy and became a mass movement only after the first World War.

Under Gandhi's leadership, local units were established. These were led by educated persons distributed throughout the rural periphery, who acted as representatives of the peasants (J.M. Brown, 1972; Embree, 1972; Morris—Jones, 1976). Thus, many encounters between peasants and their landlords or British authorities were mediated by local leaders of the Congress Party, and a functional power base for party support was thereby built.

The Congress Party then utilized four strategies to sustain its leading political position. Firstly, it created an effective balance between particularistic and more universalistic political representation. Secondly, it created a balance between local and central powers, limiting the autonomy of both regional and central elites. Thirdly, it manipulated nationalist symbols of legitimation to counterbalance provincial interests. Lastly, it balanced populist and elitist strategies as well as political and administrative methods in order to mobilize public loyalty and support (Hartmann, 1971; Kochanek, 1968; Nicholson, 1968:306ff; Weiner, 1967:30–41).

The Congress Party served as an intermediary agent for various groups and on various levels. On the district level, for example, Congress committees balanced the demands of different primordial groups, thereby mitigating pressures before they reached the national level. The efficiency of these committees was generally a function of incorporating traditional principles and modern methods of organization (Weiner, 1967:163ff). More specifically, these lesser party leaders acted principally as mediators between the local populace and the national political and economic markets (Kockanek, 1968). A case study of the Belgaum district by Weiner (1967) bears this out. He found that representatives elected to the state legislature also acted as important expeditors. Indeed, they were less concerned with performing their roles as lawmakers than with manipulating social relationships. In this way, they served their clients as well as aggregated power. Thus, the role of party leader was expanded to include political, quasi-judicial, and administrative functions. In fact, whether or not a prospective candidate was a skillful expeditor became a criterion for party selection (Weiner, 1967:258).

Weiner distinguished four necessary mediatory attributes of political leaders in the Congress Party: not being a party to the dispute, high status, sufficient power to ensure that the disputants accept his advice, and an understanding of the background and complexities of the case in question (1967:267). Thus, it may be inferred that a leader can only serve as a mediator if he is simultaneously involved in a given dispute and taking a third-party stand; that is, he must be a dual man.

Equally important is the fact that the party leaders did not act as individuals but rather operated institutions. They set up semi-official bodies and voluntary associations,

> serving as intermediates between villagers and local bureaucrats, finding employment for local youths, managing local government bodies, conducting social welfare activities, serving as mediators in village disputes, [and] organizing election campaigns (Weiner, 1967:85).

The local Congress Party leaders and their institutions utilized multiple and sometimes antagonistic methods to mobilize support. For example, in the

1968 Bombay civil elections Congress Party candidates not only made concrete promises to certain sections of the community (e.g., with respect to
housing and the water supply) but also symbolized them in traditional terms.
Furthermore, candidates were chosen not only on a merit basis but also according to their primordial affiliations (caste, language, religion) (Badhei and
Rao, 1968:8–10, 19).

In general, then, the Congress Party institutionalized its mediatory functions through the establishment of informal agents to deal with disputes, thus
offsetting dependence solely on personal charisma. Traditional and modern
elements were "fused" in both urban and rural areas by these agents, whose
services were officially institutionalized.

The Congress Party did not eliminate the strains between centrifugal and
centripetal forces but rather institutionalized them. In other words, bargaining among particularistic powers was structured into the party framework. As
will be shown later, Mrs. Gandhi attempted to alter this structure in order to
gain power during the emergency period (1975–1977). Actually, this very
change diminished both her power and legitimacy. It seems that the Janata
Party established itself on the same principles as the traditional Congress
Party, and its success in 1977 might be partially attributed to this framework;
it is still too early, however, to analyze the phenomenon in depth.

2. *Primordially oriented parties.* Besides the corporate Congress Party,
and perhaps to a lesser degree following the establishment of the Janata Party
(1977), the Indian political system includes small parties representing religious
and ethnic sentiments. These parties can be defined as retail traders that
mobilize primordial sentiments (usually combined with some class interests)
in a more or less institutionalized way. On the right are two major examples:
the Jan Sangh and the Muslim League. Both are somewhat conservative with
leadership originating in the middle and upper classes. Another primordially
oriented party which will be discussed is the Scheduled Caste Federation.

The Jan Sangh has mobilized primordial sentiment generally based on traditional commitments in order to ensure its power and influence (Baxter,
1971; Umapathy, 1968). As a result, it has generally been able to mobilize
some support from all classes. Analysis of its sources of power reveals that it
is successful in areas where orthodox Hinduism is still strong, social reform
movements have not developed, and traditional, religious, and cultural values
are deeply respected (Dasgupta and Morris-Jones, 1976). The party received
no support whatsoever in areas where powerful anti-Brahmin movements have
shaken the caste system and industrialization has stimulated modernization
(Jhangiani, 1967:171). However, it is often supported by low castes, which
exploit its anti-Muslim postures to promote their own economic interests.

The party's use of parochial sentiments to mobilize power can be viewed
as an attempt to link "traditional" and "modern" patterns of affiliation. The
utilization of primordial symbols in politics has not only increased clashes in

the system but has also enabled various middle and lower castes to mobilize power and to promote their interests. In that sense, the Jan Sangh can be seen as mediating between primordial affiliations and national politics. Even its merger with the Janata Party in the 1977 elections did not change its basic functions.

The Muslim League, the other major primordial party, was established at the beginning of the century (1906) and became the leading power among the Indian Muslims prior to partition. During this period the League had the support of most voters in provinces with a Muslim majority (Bengal, Punjab, Sind, and the Northwest Frontier Provinces). At first, the League declared its loyalty to Indian nationalism (the Lucknow Pact, 1916). However, from the 1920s increasing divergence of interests between the Hindu-dominated Congress Party and the Muslim League became apparent and was later transformed into a deep conflict. During the 1930s growing communal problems further accentuated the split between Muslims and Hindus; consequently, the League lost all confidence in the Congress Party and in the 1940s officially adopted a resolution favoring the establishment of a separate Muslim state (Kothari, 1970a:70). After the partition of the Indian subcontinent the Muslim League lost much of its political appeal, which led to increasing factionalism in the Muslim community (Ray, 1978).

Despite its reduced power, the Muslim League (and other Muslim factions) has been serving almost as a lobby in the Indian Parliament and within some of the political parties, particularly the ruling Congress Party. The Muslim League can be considered mediatory in nature in that through its alliances with other parties and its promotion of religious interests it has linked the Muslim population with other parts of Indian society.

The Scheduled Caste Federation and its successor, the Republican Party, are additional illustrations of all-India organizations in which primordial sentiments and class interests have been used for political mobilization. Despite the fact that most of the major political parties have their own organizations for the harijans, these castes have turned to independent associations in order to increase their bargaining power. Such organizations have served to increase their participation in the Indian national movement and yet to augment splits on a caste basis.

What is important in this respect is the coexistence of ascriptive arrangements, such as reserved seats in the assemblies for the scheduled castes, and of competitive politics. It is this combination which has enabled primordial associations to fill a mediatory function.

3. *Class-oriented parties.* While most primordial associations also contain class elements, their basis of mobilization is not a purely economic one. Class-oriented parties, on the other hand, generally contain different primordial sentiments but stress class interests. They work as institutionalized mechanisms for mediating between such interests and state and national politics. The

major blocs that fall into this category are the Swatantra, the Socialists, and the Communists.

The Swatantra is an urban, middle-class party which exploits both class slogans and traditional symbols in order to gain a more popular basis of support. The party was established in 1959 as a counter-force to the Communist Party, aimed at developing laissez faire economic enterprise (Erdman, 1967; Hartmann, 1971:149ff). In this way, the party represented middle-class interests. This class pattern was mitigated somewhat when the Swatantra joined the Janata Party in the 1977 elections and the government subsequently established. In this new posture, the party's intermediary power was probably increased.

The Socialist Party can be described as representing multiple interests of intellectuals, groups of industrial workers, government employees, and even peasant groups. Historically, it can be traced to the establishment of the Praja Socialist Party (1952), which was the result of a merger between the intellectual-dominated Socialist Party and the Kisan Mazdoor Praja (a peasant party established by A. Kripalani). As a result of the many different interests existing within its framework, the party has undergone a number of splits and has reappeared under varying names (e.g., the Somyukta Socialist Party, established in 1962). In the 1977 elections, the Socialists joined in the founding of the Janata Party and later participated in the government. Despite the numerous forms the party has assumed, it can still be consistently viewed as a tool used by certain groups of educated and workers to negotiate with other interest groups and the center. In that sense, it has a special mediatory standing.

The Communist Party (or parties) is perhaps the most important lower-class oriented agent in India politics. Since its establishment in the 1920s it has represented the discontented strata (B.S. Gupta, 1972; Karnik, 1957; Lieten, 1975, 1977; Overstreet and Windmiller, 1959). Prior to independence it stressed class interests and negated primordial affiliations and the concept of nationhood; consequently, it drew little support from the traditional periphery. After independence, however, the party extended its influence and power by utilizing some primordial affiliations and transforming them into class interests. It thus cultivated the support of fluid groups, such as landless peasants, workers, and some members of the middle classes who lacked opportunities for mobility (Dasgupta and Morris-Jones, 1976:291–292; Field and Franda, 1974).

The unique character of the Communist parties can be explained by their patterns of mobilization, which often change from non-institutionalized to institutionalized and vice versa. It is the transfer from one method to another (or rather their fusion) which explains the ability of these parties to mediate between the discontented and the center. It seems that the almost dialectical utilization of both non-institutionalized and institutionalized methods of political pressure, which well serves the interests of the Communist leadership, has been the reason why a more revolutionary trend has been avoided in India.

Despite the overt efforts of the Communist parties to utilize discontent to provoke unrest and revolutionize the peasantry and workers, their success has been quite limited. The relatively negligible inclination to adopt Communism under conditions of poverty, such as those found in India, has posed an enigma to scholars. The situation has usually been explained by the caste system, the feudal, non-fluid structure of the rural areas, the weakness and apathy of peripheral groups, and the oppressive methods of the regime. All these interpretations, however, can only partially explain the phenomenon. To understand how peripheral deprivation has been channelled and institutionalized (rather than revolutionized) (see Scott, 1976; Wolf, 1973), it is necessary to examine the conditions under which the Communist parties have operated in India.

Since the foundation of the Communist Party the major topic of debate and provocator of party splits within its leadership has been the question of whether to employ revolutionary or institutionalized measures (Lieten, 1975). During the late fifties this dichotomy was accentuated by the increase in national economic problems. In 1964 the party formally split into two groups: the CPI, a moderate Communist party basically representing small cultivators, and the CPI(M), a more radical Marxist party, drawing greater support from tenants and landless laborers (Franda, 1971; Ghosh, 1975; Hardgrave, 1974:176; A.K. Roy, 1975; Zagoria, 1971). Although competition between the two parties has often increased non-institutionalized behavior (as in the case of the Naxalites), most of the discontent and revolutionary potential in the country continues to be expressed through institutionalized channels.

Even though the Communist parties use institutionalized politics differently, their strategies can be analyzed in terms of the same three-stage model. In the first stage the parties accentuate class conflicts and are openly subversive, encouraging violent struggles whenever possible. The use of such non-institutional methods then provokes strong reactions from the government as well as an unfavorable reponse from some peripheral groups within the parties. In the third stage, in an attempt to adapt themselves to the above pressures, the Communists often take more institutionalized approaches, such as the creation of broad political fronts and pressure groups, the mobilization of political power based on primordial interests, the legal infiltration of state and local administration, and the exploitation of government institutions to promote their own interests (Varkey, 1974:4—5).[5]

In general, the Communists have been ambivalent toward the use of revolutionary methods. This can be explained by three factors. Firstly, some party leaders have been reluctant to risk their position in the established order. Secondly, some of the potential for extremism has been absorbed into the well-institutionalized structure in three different ways: (1) the ideological

extremism of some of the historical national leaders (Tilak, Lajpat Rai, Aurobindo Ghose) and their movements absorbed large portions of the discontented strata and thereby removed some of the potential bases of support of
the Communist parties; (2) less extreme ideologies, which mobilized support
by utilizing traditional concepts (such as those of Gandhi), successfully competed with the class ideology of the Communists; and (3) the factional structure which has dominated Indian politics (discussed later) has enhanced
particularistic patterns of mobilization and lessened the appeal of the Communists' universal class-oriented ideology. Finally, the internal makeup of the
Communist parties, including such groups as the peasants, workers, and
educated, has created a need for compromise and indirectly forced the Communists to adopt more moderate methods. Consequently, the Communist
parties have combined revolutionary slogans with mostly institutionalized
means. It is this combination of antagonistic elements that has enabled these
parties to serve in a mediatory capacity, linking the discontented to institutionalized politics. This characteristic distinguishes the Communists from
the semi- and extra-institutional movements discussed later in this chapter.

4. *Communal parties.* As illustrated earlier (Ch. 2), Indian ethnic and
religious diversity greatly overlaps local primordial differences. Communal
parties link the ethnic-linguistic periphery to the main political center. This
manipulation of local and primordial sentiments and interests has enlarged
the mediatory power of the party system. By mobilizing regional, multi-caste,
and multi-class interests, these parties have promoted the collective identities
of certain minorities. This very fact has enabled them to interact in a more
symmetric way with the majority or the center. Probably the most important
example of such parties are the Akali Dal in Punjab, established by the Sikhs
in the 1950s, and the DMK in Tamil Nadu.

The main aim of the Akali Dal party has been to revive and promote the
Sikh tradition and identity (Hartmann, 1971:210ff). Its power in Punjab has
been based on its historical role in the Sikh movement, financial support from
wealthy Sikh families, and its control over certain traditional social networks.
Because it is composed of different primordial groups, it has often been
subject to internal conflicts and divisions (as was the case in 1962, when the
Sant and Master groups split up), but none serious enough to threaten its
control of the state. In the 1977 elections the party received about forty percent of the votes in Punjab and was able to enhance its influence over the
state government.

The Tamil political organization, the DMK, was established in 1949. In its
early stages it aimed at establishing an independent Dravidian state. After the
party leadership attained control of the state government its goals were
changed; it then worked to promote the Dravidian identity and to increase its
bargaining power with the central government. The DMK has essentially been
a middle-class organization, which has also successfully mobilized the support

of lower classes and castes through ethnic sentiments (Hartmann, 1971:172ff; Walch, 1976).

The process by which Dravidian sentiments were channelled into the main-stream can be seen within the context of certain periods in the history of South India. Early in the century the Tamils founded an anti-Brahmin move-ment and built up a Justice party organization. Ethnic identification was established on the basis of Dravidian sentiments awakened in the South (ex-pressed in leaflets such as the anti-Brahmin Manifesto of 1916, perhaps the most extreme document of dissent in India) and directed against the Aryan "invaders" or the center of society (Irschick, 1969:358ff). Various clashes ensued with the dominant North and the institutions of the Indian national movement. These encounters strengthened the self-confidence of the Tamils, reinforced their solidarity, and won the respect of other Indian groups. From that point, the DMK became the major mediatory device between the Dravidian entity and the center.

After independence the conflict with the center was intensified. Tamil power was strengthened through a fundamental reconstruction of its culture and history. Specific Tamil institutions were developed which enabled the Dravidians to bargain symmetrically with the center and to gain a better distribution of resources from the Union. This Tamil parochialism seems to have been politically converted in such a way as to have helped their absorp-tion (in a relatively egalitarian manner) into society. Thus, after aggregating power, the Dravidians were willing to recognize national symbols and insti-tutions. For example, the Tamil Writer's Association has stressed the need to study, in addition to the Tamil culture, all of India's religions, philosophies, and national figures (including Tagore, for instance) (*Bulletin of the National Integration Unit* No. 12/5/69, Annexure IV, p. 33).

The DMK gained political control in Madras and Tamil Nadu in March 1968. As a ruling party, it had to meet all the problems faced by the non-ethnic parties on the state level and to assume universal orientations. Thus, in their official positions, DMK leaders (e.g., Mr. Annadurai) found it useful to declare their allegiance to the Indian constitution and its basic secular values. However, while officially endorsing the fundamental consensual values, they utilized them to legitimize their own particularistic demands, including official recognition of the Tamil language in Tamil Nadu. As a result of its assuming control over the state, the DMK became more responsible in its en-counters with the center, which eventually reduced separatist trends among the Tamils (Jagannathan, 1968:8).

In general, one may conclude that the communal parties have acted as agents collecting various provincial sentiments or interests under one roof and channelling them into modern politics. This very mediatory process has contributed to the legitimation and integration of Indian society but, at the same time, has slowed down the process of social change. Communal parties are distinguished from class-oriented parties by their use of different sources of legitimation and political strategies. Their use of institutionalized, ethnic loyalties makes them a unique tool for mediation between center and periphery.

5. *Semi- and extra-institutional movements.* In a society experiencing scarcity, there is always hardship and deprivation as well as discontent which can neither be absorbed nor mediated by the more or less institutionalized bodies. In Indian society this socio-economic deprivation has been politically manipulated through: (1) independent mobilization of voting power operating outside the established parties but within the party system;[6] (2) redistributive movements, which seek to alter the distribution of wealth, utilizing semi-institutionalized, voluntaristic, and persuasive means (e.g., the Bhoodan Gramdan movement) (Oommen, 1971); (3) protest movements acting on an ad hoc basis and using semi-institutional means, such as student protests or strikes; and (4) extra-institutional movements organized along class, cross-primordial lines, aimed at transforming both the rules of the existing order and its patterns of distribution of wealth and power through every available means (B. Dasgupta 1974).[7] (The Naxalite movement in West Bengal can be cited in this context.)

All four categories include movements not embodied in any registered party. Common to these groups is the fact that they increase conflict in Indian society by their frequent use of semi-violent tactics (Aiyar, 1967).

The first three categories are semi- or quasi-institutionalized bodies and include disadvantaged or deprived groups such as the Jharkand Party in Bihar, the Republican Party and the Peasants and Workers Party in Maharashtra, and some parts of the Scheduled Caste Federation (which operated under different names before independence) that were officially institutionalized in 1957 and later participated in the Janata government. The last category often contains temporary extra-institutional associations, such as the Anand Marg, the RSS, deprived class associations, and various Muslim organizations.

The Anand Marg is a militant Hindu association which claimed about 100,000 members in 1970. This movement has been willing to use almost every possible means to maintain the dominancy of the old Hindu traditions. Until the State of Emergency (1975–1977), the movement held a semi-institutional position that enabled it to legally express extreme sentiments while allowing central control over its whole movement.

The Rashtriya Swayamasevak Sangh (RSS), founded by Dr. K.B. Hedgewar in 1925, aimed at the revival of the Hindu religion and the "glorification of the Hindu race and culture." It was established as a Hindu counter-force to the Muslim League and developed during the forties as a major tool for the absorption of Hindu militancy (Baxter, 1971: Chs. II, III; Curran, 1951). RSS militancy converted traditional sentiments into modern political tools (which probably explains how it largely became institutionalized and was able to support the Janata Party in the 1977 elections).

Extra-institutionalized organizations are also found among the Muslims of India. The most salient have been the Jamaat-e-Islamic Hind, Jammiyyat-al Ulama-i-Hind, Tabligh-e-Jammat, Kul Hind Tameer-e-Millat, and Majlis-e-Mushhawarat (Friedmann, 1976). All these groups have aimed at promoting Muslim interests and strengthening their identity in India after partition (Hartmann, 1971; Kothari, 1970a:246). While reflecting the most extreme anti-Hindu sentiments, they have also mediated between Muslim tradition and the Indian secular state. It is therefore not surprising that the Indian government has often supported these movements unofficially (Friedmann, 1976: 210–211). It seems that through this extra- or semi-institutional expression of extremism some symbiosis of Hindu and Muslim culture has been promoted.

Apparently the existence of semi-institutional movements, while increasing clashes in the short run, has decreased the revolutionary potential in Indian society in the long run. Although most of these movements have occasionally used anti-institutional means to promote their interests and have even incited rebellion or seizure of state power, they have also provided Indian society with a tool with which to mediate between the system and various marginal groups. In fact, their mere existence has forced the center to take extreme demands into account. Thus, paradoxically, as articulators of discontent and deprivation, such groups may assume the role of mediatory systems. "It is precisely the increasing dispersal of the political system that is bringing about a mobilization of the periphery and its consequent integration into national politics" (Kothari, 1970a:198). In other words, extreme violent groups have often acted not as agents who increase clashes, but as institutions through which various types of frustrations have been absorbed into the system (Kothari, 1970a:247–249).

Conclusions

As has been shown, the party system, together with semi- and extra-institutional groups, has reinforced three almost dialectical stages in the process of integration on the political level:

1. In the first stage splits among various primordial groups and/or social classes are accentuated. Each stresses its own identity and establishes its own institutions as instruments of internal solidarity and for the purpose of bargaining with the center and other groups in society.

2. Once these groups achieve solidarity, project a positive and worthy self-image, and are awarded social recognition, they reach the stage of symmetry in their relations with other groups. Since in symmetrical relationships no one group is strong enough to impose its will on others, various groups possessing nearly equal resources reach agreement on general, universal rules.

3. In the final stage, the more or less different but relatively equal groups develop common institutions based on balanced reciprocity and a transcendence of primordial and/or class divisions. These institutions, acting as bar-

gaining arenas, often function in terms of what may be considered a statistical average of the power of the groups involved. Not only has the spectrum of representation been widened through this process but varying interests have also been channelled into the very core of society.

One may characterize political processes in India as a dynamic balance of activities between extra-, quasi-, and intra-institutional movements. It is this dynamism which underlies mediatory processes. Generally speaking, the major phases in the mediation process are: firstly, the use of extreme slogans and extra-institutional tactics, usually prior to election time; and secondly, when advantages are gained or the election won, the establishment of a coalition or alliance between the new ruling parties and some other groups that together attempt to use institutional means (e.g., the legislature) to promote social change. In this context, elections can be defined as mechanisms aimed at the institutionalization of conflict and the allocation of power to different groups. The electoral system mediates between groups by encouraging competition within well-codified boundaries (Bhalla, 1973; Dasgupta and Morris-Jones, 1976:Ch.V).

Indian elections, which have usually increased conflict as well as a sense of separate identity, have also somehow provided an arena for such struggles. This perhaps explains Palmer's findings that seventy-five percent of his sample of Indian voters perceived elections as necessary, and about sixty-six percent felt the same regarding political parties (1975:255–256).

The fact that the Indian party system has been able to keep conflict within institutionalized boundaries may also be explained by a factor which has not been considered until now: its special pattern of organization whereby most parties and political movements are composed of small groups, factions, and caste associations.

FACTIONAL POLITICS AND CASTE ASSOCIATIONS

The intermediary process in India cannot be fully understood without also referring to the lower echelons of politics, namely, the caste associations and political factions.[8] These organizations can be viewed as forming the lower levels of the political pyramid. Whereas the various political parties are situated on the middle strata and connect local particularistic groups with state or national politics, local primordial or factional groups mobilize the support of the man in the street and operate as lobbies on the local and national political levels (Oren, 1973).

A caste association can be defined as a quasi-interest group based on primordial affiliation. It has a dual character in that it embodies a conscious attempt to utilize ascriptive loyalties for functional political action.[9] From a more theoretical viewpoint, caste associations are based on a combination of "mechanic" and "organic" patterns of solidarity, the former operating internally as a cohesive force and converted into the latter in local and national politics. Such factional groups are characterized by their ability to act in terms of small, particularistic, almost private interests, which they convert into political power. This conversion is achieved with the help of lesser leaders (Morris-Jones, 1976), who interfuse different codes and translate them into language easily understood by higher-ranking politicians and common people alike.

Of value to our discussion is not the mere existence of caste or factional groups, nor the non-exclusive coexistence of caste and class elements within them, but rather their intermediary nature. The degree to which a caste association can be said to fulfill a mediatory role depends on its ability to fuse antagonistic principles and to convert prestige, economic assets, interests, primordial sentiments, and demographic numbers into political power. Caste associations and factional groups are pervasive agents of both change and stagnation, since they manipulate the traditional structure in a modern organizational pattern and sharpen primordial and class splits. In fact, their political flexibility is explained by their rigid traditional framework. In that sense, factional groups may be defined as agents of traditionalization of modernity rather than of modernity of tradition (see G.R. Gupta, 1978).

It is generally accepted that caste associations and *jati* alliances have by and large provided an infrastructure for political mobilization (Carter, 1974; R. Roy, 1970; Rudolph and Rudolph, 1967). Local *jatis* have traditionally been the focus of relatively homogeneous interests because of the similar occupations, prestige, and wealth of their members. In addition, *jati* affiliation has been based on institutionalized primordial sentiments. These two factors, together with the internal collective organization of the *jati*, based on the caste-*panchayat*, has made caste affiliation an efficient and inexpensive device for mobilization of political power.

The caste associations have been essentially utilized on three levels of Indian politics. On the village level they operate as a *jati*, mobilizing support in a patronage pattern (Breman, 1974; Burkhart, 1975; Carter, 1974:5; Lynch, 1976). On the regional level alliances are made between *jatis*, each of which articulates the power of a specific primordial group. On the national or state level such coalitions are converted into interest groups, that is, factions or lobbies which bargain for the benefit of their members within political parties. In that sense, Indian politics can somewhat be described as a gradual or stratified structure in which local coalitions merge into state alliances, which, in turn, are transformed into national ones (Carter, 1974: Ch.7).

Alliances on the local level (as in the party system) are established on an ad hoc basis through agreement among lesser leaders and active caste members and through relations established between them and potential supporters (Carter, 1974:6–8; Morris-Jones, 1976). The mandate of a leader largely depends on his ability to create such alliances and to buy or sell voting power. Here we come to the core of Indian factional politics: the political system is based on the unstable coalition of stable groups and on the flexible implementation of inflexible, diffused groups. The factions negotiate among themselves and with state and national leaders in a rational way in an attempt to maximize their profits (Carras, 1972; D.B. Miller, 1975; Rastogi, 1975).

Certain studies have pointed to the fact that the politicization of the traditional castes has changed their internal structure as well as their relationships with other castes (Alexander, 1968; Beteille, 1969; Kothari, 1970a, 1970b; Srinivas, 1969). Their internal structure has become based on a combination of primordial and non-primordial criteria and, as a result, has become more fluid. The following is a brief historical survey of the major steps in the politicization of the caste system.

During the first phase of development most caste associations were organized in a Guru-Shishy patronage pattern of relationship (Rastogi, 1975: 4–5). With increasing political fluidity, the associations became loosely structured and more temporary in nature. In addition, they lost their broader meaning and became less powerful mechanisms for controlling their members. At the same time, however, they became more flexible and therefore served as efficient bargaining devices.

The development of caste associations as a political instrument was partially due to the competitive election system which was instituted in the 1920s. The formal guarantee of equal rights of representation (still limited in degree) gave a great amount of potential political strength to the rural population. Utilization of the primordial groups proved to be the easiest way to convert this potential into actual power, and caste associations were the natural result. The establishment of such organizations reinforced the openness of the system and increased caste conflicts but at the same time enhanced the internal transformation of caste alliances, making them more fluid entities. The Nadars provide the most common illustration of this model (Hardgrave, 1969).

Members of a large *jati* traditionally known as Chanans, the Nadars were concentrated in the Madras presidency and in the southern part of Travancore. They were considered a *jati* of low status (i.e., not twice-born). In the first decades of the nineteenth century the Chanans became a successful commercial class in Madras because of an increase in economic opportunities. In the 1830s the Chanans tried to promote their status by changing their style of dress, and in 1858 the Governor of Madras "granted their women permission to wear cloth over their breasts and shoulders... but not like women of higher castes" (Rudolph and Rudolph, 1967: 38–39). The clothes they wore signified their inferior status and were not consistent with their economic resources, which were sometimes greater than those of the twice-born castes (Brahmins, Kshatriyas, and Vaishyas). To resolve this inconsistency, they began to claim different origins. The 1891 census classified them as a polluting caste but also reported that many of them claimed to be Kshatriyas. At this time they unsuccessfully tried to adopt new rituals and rules of behavior in order to be accorded a new status. The inconsistency was not resolved until the period from 1910 to 1917, when the Chanans became politically organized to promote their general welfare. Their power increased after the Montague-Chelmsford reforms. Chanan policy was to further their children's education and thereby achieve more recognition in traditional and modern terms alike. In 1921 the Chanans succeeded in officially changing their name to Nadar and gaining public recognition of their new status.

One may conceptualize the three-stage conversion process of the Nadars in which, firstly, wealth was aggregated; secondly, it was converted into education and political power; and lastly, these resources were converted into social prestige. One may conclude that the Nadars' mobility was achieved through a fusion of the traditional forms of sanskritization and modern techniques of achievement.

More recent research on the rise of caste associations, focusing on Maharashtra from the turn of the century, reveals that, while the situation is similar to that described above, the process of mobilization has been simplified since independence (Omvedt, 1976). Acquisition of political power has become an almost sufficient condition for mobility, and the conversion of power and wealth into prestige, which was common traditionally, is no longer necessary. In other words, the cultural processes of Brahminization and sanskritization (transforming power and wealth into prestige) as discussed by Srinivas (1969) are no longer the sole means of mobility.

Structural change in Indian society has been one of the most important results of the increased politicization of traditional castes. Beteille astutely observes:

> The system thus becomes flexible in two ways: firstly, in any given context the meaning of "caste" is increasingly stretched and secondly, the new vertical divisions based on income, occupation and education allow by their very nature a certain degree of individual mobility (1969:73).

Structurally speaking, what Beteille describes is a dialectical process in which the use of primordial affiliations diminishes their strength.

This process of integration is similar to that described earlier in the party system. In the first stage extreme emphasis on particularism leads to a securer sense of identity and self-pride. In the second, after some power has been aggregated, the caste begins negotiations with the governing powers. Integration occurs through negotiations based on a more symmetric relationship.

It is crucial that relationships both between and within castes have changed through this process. The manipulation of ascriptive groups in politics increased political awareness among those who first initiated caste associations. The following generation departed from such communalism and developed more universal organizational and political reforms. Furthermore, while the first generation made symbolic demands, its successors became more concrete and pragmatic in their orientation.

The politicization of caste associations may be explained by their traditional structure. An additional factor is the existence of educated representatives rooted in the *jati* system and having a good grasp of modern concepts. This group has utilized caste associations for its own benefits. Educated leaders have used primordial factions in the rural areas both as agencies for mobilizing support for all-India parties and as diffuse pressure groups within those parties (Weiner, 1967:150). On the national level the caste association has been a "conscious creation of the urban-educated political elite seeking institutional bases and numerical strength for their support" (Mayer, 1967:36).

As a result of the elites' interest in promoting caste asssociations, laws providing protective discrimination have been extended. This has made the Indian political system more ascriptive. Consequently, while serving the interests of the educated, factional politics has forced elites to take popular demands into account and therefore has provided India with an efficient tool for reducing the distance between the center and the rural periphery. The result, of course, is that the position of the upper castes has been threatened. While elites continue to enjoy more advantages of the system in the short run, their privileged status is gradually diminishing.

The power of caste associations has, however, been weakened by their recent spread and division into smaller units (Kothari, 1970b; Rastogi, 1975; Saraswathi, 1974), which has served to increase the splits in Indian society. The emergence of small factions has made each of them more representative, but diminished their bargaining power. Of course, this process has enabled the ruling center to divide and rule efficiently and has therefore increased its power.

The increasing fragmentation into caste associations has accelerated the centrifugal processes in Indian society to such a degree that it may be having more of a disintegrative effect than an integrative one. However, it does seem that this process is somewhat countered when factions unify at the local level and establish alliances.

To conclude, the conversion of primordial-factional groups into more modern associations can be considered a mechanism of socio-cultural transformation. In India this tool has been used mainly to increase both political fluidity and particularistic trends (Saraswathi, 1974). It seems that the utilization of primordial groups in politics has mediated their demands and has therefore institutionalized and diminished extremism. At the same time, however, the process of change has been slowed down.

Perhaps the most significant factor which has allowed the utilization of *jatis* for political action is the availability of educated lesser leaders who have organized these caste associations (Brass, 1965; J.M. Brown, 1972; Carter, 1974:7; Morris-Jones, 1976). The articulation of caste associations and factions in a free market system has enabled the Indian elites to maintain diversity while politically institutionalizing it. Furthermore, the partial overlapping between class, caste, and power has allowed elites to manipulate both interests and sentiments within one framework. At the same time, a more symmetrical type of political bargaining has developed. In other words, the whole system has become more reciprocal in nature, contributing to its legitimation and integration.

FEDERAL ARRANGEMENTS

As has been repeatedly shown above, Indian society can be defined on the most general level as a corporate entity in which various groups (e.g., parties, factions, castes) act as almost shareholders. Such a corporate principle also operates on the inter-state level. The Indian Union is divided into twenty-two states and nine union territories, which are organized as a federal system and enjoy a considerable degree of autonomy with regard to internal affairs (I. Narain, 1976).[10] The federal system can also be viewed as a mechanism mediating between center and periphery, and between centripetal and centrifugal forces.

The essence of the federal corporate system (as opposed to the system found in the United States) is that it is based on primordial (linguistic and religious) units rather than on geographical, economic, or administrative entities.

Neither the British provincial system nor the sovereign political entities underlay the emergence of the Indian federal system (Gallagher et al., 1973; Santhanam, 1960). Rather, it was introduced by Indian educated elites shortly after independence in an attempt to counter separatist trends. The major aim was to grant the most densely populated, homogeneous regions an opportunity to maintain their particular identity while at the same time providing a common political market for negotiations among such groups. In other words, the federal corporate system has institutionalized division into sub-cultures, giving each the opportunity to express its identity through its receipt of political sovereignty. This dualism probably explains how and why federalism functions in India. The arrangement has enabled the center, on the one hand, to control India's sizeable population, a feat which would probably have been otherwise unfeasible, and, on the other, to institutionalize the clash between the states and the center.

Horizontally, federalism divides India into units of equal status; vertically, it enables local leaders, representing various particularistic interests, to exert pressure upon the center (Rosen, 1966:104). Consequently, a considerable amount of competition has occurred among the state governments, and between them and the center. This competition has been institutionalized in the federal system, in which each state, as well as the Union government, acts within loosely defined constitutional boundaries. In this system centrifugal trends are often countered by centripetal bodies. For instance, the central administration, including the governors nominated by the central government, has constantly intervened in state politics and central commissions for planning have acted to accommodate resource distribution among the states.

The power of centripetal and centrifugal forces has been constitutionally equalized. Article 257/1 of the Constitution states:

> The executive power of every State shall be so exercised as not to impede or prejudice the exercise of the executive power of the Union, and the executive power of the Union shall extend to the giving of such directions to a State as may appear to the Government of India to be necessary for that purpose (quoted in Peaslee, 1974:287).

Empirically, with reference to resource allocation, confrontation between the two trends has been mitigated by a federal policy which treats the states in an almost egalitarian manner (Santhanam, 1960; S. Sarkar, 1972). This policy aims at reducing tension among the states and, to some extent, among the principal groups within each state. Equal distribution of resources is often quite irrational when considered from a purely economic standpoint, since it hardly takes into account relative advantage and natural and social opportunities (Rosen, 1966). From a social point of view, however, such a policy of compromise has helped to institutionalize clashes.

In recent years there has been a shift toward a more rational, less egalitarian pattern of resource allocation and a resultant change in the relationship between centrifugal and centripetal forces. An examination of the distribution of resources clearly reveals that much effort has been expended on the part of the individual states to enlarge their share in accordance with their tax potential. The rich states (e.g., Gujarat, Maharashtra, and West Bengal), which pay more taxes per capita, have been pressuring the center for a less "progressive" tax system (K.N. Reddy, 1975). Their efforts have been partially successful; fewer preferential policies of investment and development have been adopted. As a result, the gap between rich and poor states has grown. This shift reflects the fact that the center has acquired more and more power – so much so that it virtually controls the states. Hence, the integration of the diversified states has become more and more difficult. At the moment, however, the federal arrangement can still be considered a political tool through which centrifugal and centripetal trends in Indian society are coordinated. In that sense, Indian federalism is quite similar to that found in the West (Friedrich, 1968); the difference between the two systems is in the nature of the centrifugal and centripetal forces as well as in the method of equalizing them.

CONCLUSIONS

The present chapter has been devoted to India's political bridging mechanisms, which can essentially be characterized as working on three different levels: along caste, political party, and state lines. These mechanisms are based on antagonistic codes of action (i.e., they operate on the basis of primordial affiliations but relate to universalistic criteria), and it is essential to note that such dual criteria have been fused operationally and have not preserved their differentiated basis. In this way, such mechanisms have not only had an integrative effect but have also acted to decelerate the process of change, especially in the economic sphere.

Theoretically what unifies all three phenomena discussed in this chapter (political parties, factional and caste politics, and federal arrangements) is the fact that they are simultaneously manipulated by dual principles and by systems and counter-systems. Thus, they are able to contain antagonistic structural components and processes. This largely explains the mediatory function they assume in coping with such opposing forces as centrifugal and centripetal movements, local and national politics, elitism and populism, and a dominant caste model and factional pluralism. In this way, disintegrative forces have often been transformed into integrative ones.

NOTES

1. For a general discussion of party systems, see, for example, La Palombara, 1974; Ostrogorski, 1902; Sartori, 1966, 1976; Schumpeter, 1950.

2. There are three indicators of weak political ties in India: the rapid shift of loyalties and support by local groups and leaders from one party to another; splits within parties; and the significant number of votes for non-established parties (e.g., independents), comprising about thirty percent of the electorate from 1949 until the 1971 elections (Dasgupta and Morris-Jones, 1976:194–195).

3. Thus, for example, Dasgupta and Morris-Jones found that between 1952 and 1969 there were 110 such alignments participating in elections (1976:47).

4. Even the Janata Party, from a structural point of view, is just another version of what has been typical of the Indian Congress Party since the early twenties. Essentially, the Janata Party was established as a conglomeration of various groups, each having different interests. Its four-party merger (of Jan Sangh, Old Congress Party, Bharatya Lok Dal, and the Socialist Party) is actually an ad hoc alignment of various political forces assembled under one umbrella; that is, it is a corporative merger. Each of the constituent parties is based on different factions (such as RSS in the Jan Sangh) and has to reach an internal compromise before decisions can be made on the national level.

5. To illustrate this model, let us describe the case of West Bengal. In 1967 Communist tactics provoked great disorder, and chaos was averted only when the central government suspended the state constitution and restored presidential rule. After their experience with anomie and presidential rule the Communists were inclined to act in a more institutional manner as social reformers rather than as a revolutionary party; consequently, they were able to win elections. However, by assuming public office, they were brought under cross pressures; their commitment to the ideology of class struggle was challenged by the obligations and rules of participation in the constitutional government. Such a situation crystallized in June 1977 – after the CPI(M) had taken over the government in West Bengal – when clashes over the rice harvest were anticipated. Marxist party members were charged with having forcibly harvested the rice, which belonged to the landlords, for themselves. To prevent central intervention, which had already occurred twice before in the state, the party tried to convince the poor peasants to conduct their campaign within institutional boundaries.

6. Dasgupta and Morris-Jones found that independent candidates (additional candidates, including dissidents from existing national and regional parties) mobilized about 27 percent of the voting power in 1967, as compared to about 36 percent in 1952

(1976:194–195). (In 1977 it fell to 15 percent.) This might be interpreted in two opposing ways.

One explication is that extra-institutional forces tend to decrease as a function of the increased absorptive power of institutionalized parties. A second approach claims that the diminishing number of extra-institutional forces is due to the ability of the main parties to block them through non-political means (i.e., by force). In the first case a decrease in non-institutionalized politics is expected, while the latter interpretation predicts an increase of extra-political activity in the long run. In general, one may assume that the independent candidates and the dissident groups within the established parties are important mechanisms for the institutionalization of class and primordial conflicts in India.

7. In his study on Bengal, D.L. Sheth (1975) found that radicalism was not identified with extremism. Although there was strong disapproval of government policy concerning land reform and redistribution of property as well as a marked preference for radical values, only a little over one fourth of his sample was willing to employ extra-institutional methods of direct action.

8. Most scholars tend to argue that Indian politics is best explained by using the *jati* model (Gould, 1969; Kothari, 1970a, 1970b; Rudolph and Rudolph, 1967; Srinivas, 1969). For example, Rudolph and Rudolph consider caste associations as the most important device for political mobilization. They distinguish between vertical patterns of mobilization (by which higher ranking leaders mobilize the support of those below them), horizontal patterns (among equals), and cross-class or cross-caste patterns (1967: 24–27). Carter also distinguishes between vertical and horizontal caste alliances. He defines the former as alliances between different classes or castes or between a "political class" and its supporters outside the political camp. The latter type is an alliance "between one political elite's leaders or (one) political class member and another" (Carter, 1974:7–8).

On the other hand, a few scholars have gone further and have defined the *jati* model in a more general way as a factional pattern of politics based on the articulation of particularistic interests (Carras, 1972; Rastogi, 1975). The existence of alliances, primordial patterns, and primordial devices of mobilization is not peculiar to India. What is unique in the Indian context is that particularistic patterns of mobilization are operated in an open bargaining type of social system. It may be noted that within this context the concept of caste is synonymous with *jati* and the two terms are used interchangeably.

9. The use of primordial ascriptive affiliations for achieving economic and political goals has been illustrated by Geertz (1963) and L. Mayhew (1968).

10. Sources on the federal system of India include Bondurant, 1958; Haqqi, 1967; Iyengar, 1974; Krishnaswami, 1964; Leonard, 1963; S. Sarkar, 1972; Setalvad, 1974.

Chapter 7

"OBJECTIVE" BRIDGING MECHANISMS

INTRODUCTION

Having discussed political bridging mechanisms, let us now turn to mechanisms purported to be above politics, assumed to provide "objective" tools for mediatory processes. It should be noted that these mechanisms are "objective" only in the sense that they are pre-determined and bound, to a greater or lesser degree, to pre-situational rules which cannot be easily or arbitrarily changed.

"Objective" mechanisms include legal institutions, the municipal *panchayat* system, the civil administration, and some of the mass media. As distinguished from political bridging mechanisms, which are rooted in and operate through the power structure, these mechanisms are purported to be neutral. In other words, they are expected to provide a universal framework or an objective third party, unidentified in principle with any particular interests and operating according to fixed rules.

This distinction, however, does not fully hold in India (and probably elsewhere) because of the lack of full differentiation between "objective" mechanisms and political institutions. As we have pointed out, the Indian system has institutionalized the synthesis of traditional and modern values of behavior at both the cultural and pragmatic levels. It is this synthesis that has enabled the legitimate utilization of antagonistic social rules and arrangements. Along the same lines, legal and administrative institutions have been interwoven with politics.

To some extent, the Indian system has encouraged the use of legal and administrative methods for political manipulation. Furthermore, modern rules and institutions have functioned in a quasi-traditional manner, while traditional mores have functioned in a modern way. Consequently, legalists and administrators have often become representatives of primordial and interest groups. This representation largely occurs within a semi-legal framework. In this way particularistic, ad hoc interests are linked with universal institutionalized rules. Although this synthesis has increased the efficiency of the "objective" institutions by making them more relevant to social interests, it has also exposed them to arbitrary influences and political pressures.

The relationship among legal, central administrative, and municipal mechanisms is as follows: The legal system provides a framework for both political and administrative processes within certain institutional boundaries. Central and state administrations connect legal and political spheres. In the municipal *panchayat* system this connection is brought down to the local level, bridging the gap between center and periphery. Finally, parts of the mass media (the press) serve to interlink various central and local elites.

Let us now examine each "objective" mechanism in turn.

LEGALITY AND LEGAL INSTITUTIONS

It is not our concern here to fully discuss the sociology of law,[1] but rather to reveal the nature of legal institutions in India and their impact in terms of legitimation and integration. Our central thesis is that these institutions have been operated as an enterprise combining political interests and statutory rules, and, as a result, they have provided an institutionalized arena for bargaining and negotiation.[2]

The concept of legality as used here will refer to the extent to which behavior in general and disputes in particular are governed by permanent, non-arbitrary rules, regardless of the sources of legitimacy and the nature of the authorities which supervise their enforcement. With such a broad definition, it is clear that legality may have different bases, such as in magical power, divine will, hereditary succession, charismatic appeal, traditional procedures, rational principles, or professional competence.

The need for legality is generally justified by the assumption that behavior cannot be regulated solely by ad hoc situational conditions or given power structures, but should be guided by relatively institutionalized rules as well. These rules are based on reciprocal codes which provide general boundaries for specific modes of behavior (Selznick, 1969). Under conditions of social change common norms become less meaningful, and it becomes extremely difficult to create and legitimize new rules. In this marginal situation a society faces the dilemma of either perpetuating common norms from the past or creating a new, less legitimized legal system.

A complete break with the past might broaden the gap between common values and habits and actual behavior. On the other hand, perpetuation of formerly accepted habits may impede the process of change. Any attempt to institutionalize rules different from, or antagonistic to, common norms decreases the former's legitimacy.

There are two ways to cope with this dilemma. The first is to minimize the extent of any rules so as to diminish the antagonism between them. In the short run, this strategy may result in a workable compromise; however, it may also lead to lawlessness. A second, less risky approach is to fuse contradictory rules by interpreting old concepts in new terms or new concepts in old terms. The fusion of different rules gives them a more universal meaning, and the more universal the legal principles, the greater the probability that the position of the parties involved will be somewhat equalized from a legal standpoint. By equalizing the positions of the negotiating parties, the whole social system becomes more open and more controlled. On the one hand, this increases the probability of conflicts; on the other, it also provides an arena for settling disputes.

With respect to the situation in India, the statutory system has been made up of a combination of traditional mores, Hindu laws (the *dharmasastra* and the Manu statutes),[3] and Islamic and Moghul rules, as well as a secular law implanted by the British. These codes, often contradictory, have sometimes been differentiated and sometimes linked. In different situations, they have provided either alternative or complementary methods of dealing with disputes (Derrett, 1979; Galanter, 1968; Mandelbaum, 1970:313). This coexistence of "traditional" customs and modern legal concepts (a fusion of "status" and "contract" in the sense of Sir Henry Maine) has led to dualism and ambiguity.

Such ambiguity characterized the Indian legal system as far back as the period of East India Company rule (R.C. Srivastava, 1971:2). With the transfer of power from Company to Crown, dualism of legal rules was accentuated. On the one hand, the British legal system was given greater weight; on the other, "pure" English law could neither work nor be enforced. Furthermore, Indian nationalists saw the combination of Western laws and Indian customs as a means of countering British influence and mobilizing public support. This was most often put into practice when political pressures forced the courts to adjust and change, or at least interpret, laws in a manner that did not run counter to traditional customs (Derrett, 1979). In this way, a fluid relationship between political and legal agents was established, giving Indian law its contextual relevancy and dynamism. The system allowed an arbitrary interpretation and effectuation of laws, which the British manipulated to their own interests (R.C. Srivastava, 1971:6).[4] The flexibility of the system also later served the interests of Indian elites, who adapted laws to local conditions.

In the late nineteenth century the British began to re-explore the possibility of shifting the judicial system into the hands of Western-educated Indians in the hope of establishing a link between the indigenous periphery and the ruling Britons. The idea had been pursued during the rule of the East India Company, when a brokerage system of low-ranking local judges or assistants (*munjih sadars, ameens*) had operated (R.C. Srivastava, 1971: Chs. 3 and 4). After that system proved inefficient, the idea of creating a mediatory class (developed from Macaulay's minute) was promoted in the early nineteenth century. By the beginning of the twentieth century, when a sufficient number of law school graduates were available, the system had become fully developed (Galanter, 1969).

While the growth in the number of Indian lawyers made law a useful device mainly for elites, it later became increasingly so for peripheral groups as well (Galanter, 1969). The familiarity of lawyers with both traditional and modern legal codes enabled them to be utilized in complementary or alternative ways according to the clients' interests. The low professional level (para-professionalism) of lawyers made them often more amenable to specific local conditions, thereby making the legal codes more applicable and workable (Morrison, 1974:43). At the same time, these factors contributed to the decline of "objective" legality and invited political interference (P.D. Sharma, 1975).

Derrett has categorized the components of the Indian legal system into four groups: (1) elements purely traditional in form and substance; (2) those traditional in form, but not in substance; (3) those traditional in substance, but not in form; and (4) those irrelevant or even hostile to tradition (i.e., completely modern) (1979:38ff).

The two middle categories can be viewed as a type of fusion. Indeed, Galanter, although referring to a failure "to replace the present legal system with revived indigenous law" after independence, acknowledges that the two systems have been somewhat fused (1972:54).

Fusion may be said to operate in four different ways. In the first, exemplified by family law, traditional mores are interwoven and even overlap modern codes. In the second, customary and modern laws are reconciled. For instance, one is allowed to take a "semi-bribe" in certain situations, albeit "not from the wrong people" and "not too much" (Derrett, 1979:49–50). In the third type traditional laws are reinterpreted and given new meaning. This is exemplified by the Cooperative Societies Act of 1912 and its modifications. Finally, modern laws are used in traditional contexts. The Dowry Prohibition Act of 1961, the Untouchability Act, and other laws abolishing customs all illustrate this type (Derrett, 1979:53). So, too, does the quasi-legalization of sanskritization in the civil courts (Srinivas, 1969).

The fused nature of the usage of Indian law has opened the way for a partial politicization of the judiciary system in the sense that lawsuits are often mediated by politicians (Derrett, 1979; Rudolph and Rudolph, 1967). This interference on the part of politicians has often led to the popularization of law and an intermingling of legal procedures and political negotiation (Bhatt, 1975). The result has been increasing adjustability on the part of the judicial system, although its "pure" legality has thereby been decreased. Consequently, the Indian court system has often been described as an incomplete or corrupted pattern of legality (Monteiro, 1966).

It must be pointed out that "corrupt" behavior (up to a certain point) can be considered a method of adjustment whereby the gap between legal and customary modes of behavior may be bridged. The existence of two or more forms of dispute settlement, together with their interweaving, leaves room for maneuvering and bargaining, with each party seeking maximal advantage (Kidder, 1974:13). Thus, the court often becomes an arena in which various political forces negotiate in an almost legitimate way. Furthermore, the system provides an institutional means for resolving conflict through a neutral third-party adjudicator. This intertwining of legal and political systems is responsible for the uniqueness of the Indian court system. Although it may be interpreted as a form of corruption and failure, it can also be viewed as a special pattern of accommodation to prevailing conditions.

The blend of political and legal spheres has sometimes catalyzed social change. The pattern in which this has occurred in Kerala since the pre-independence period was examined by Oommen (1975). First, progressive legislation concerning land redistribution is passed. Its implementation is generally made ineffective by powerful groups and individuals in the area, while judicial and administrative agents are too weak (or do not wish) to see that it is enforced. Next, politicians enter the picture, supporting implementation (a process which is sometimes accompanied by an electoral takeover of the government) and finally forcing official agents to adhere to the passed legislation. What must be stressed is that without such political interference, progressive laws, if passed at all, would merely exist on paper. This case illustrates how the convergence (rather than the differentiation) of legal, political, and economic spheres makes law effective.

Chatterjee, Singh, and Yadav (1971), who studied the impact of legislation on social change in rural Uttar Pradesh, have shown that legislation indirectly increased the peasants' aspiration and expectation levels as well as their political awareness of available choices. The researchers also found that when laws were adopted as a result of political activity, caste and peasant associations were more likely to utilize them according to their interests. The implementation of certain legislation was often highly dependent on the availability of educated leaders and political groups to intervene in the judicial decision-making process (Morris-Jones, 1976).

On the basis of the above studies, one may construct a four-stage model for law implementation. To begin with, legislation aimed at bringing about social change is initiated. Such legislation is usually rejected by established strata. Those groups in favor of the legislation then mobilize their political power. Pressure is placed on the decision-makers, constituting the third step. Finally, after legislation is passed, governmental means are employed under political constraints to reshape and enforce it. Although the order of the stages may change from time to time and from place to place, the internal logic of the process remains.

Up to now we have reviewed the process by which legality in India has been used as a mediatory mechanism. An additional factor must now be considered: the extent to which the legal system is utilized by different sections of the population.

Access to legal rights and opportunities in India is stratified to a lesser degree than would be expected considering the caste system and class differences. In fact, lower castes and classes occasionally utilize legal institutions more than upper castes (Bhatt, 1975; Cohn, 1965; Dasgupta and Morris-Jones,

1976; Kidder, 1974). This is surprising considering the high illiteracy rate and the difficult economic situation; most Indians have neither the necessary skills nor the resources to utilize the modern legal system.

It seems that three factors have contributed to the large demand for legal services. First, caste associations and educated mediators are available to almost every group. Second, politicians looking for support act as advisors, helping people bring their cases to court (Weiner, 1967). Last, there is a rather large number of available lawyers; in 1960 the ratio of lawyers to total population was 1:5,000 (Galanter, 1969). This not only makes lawyers inexpensive but also forces them to become more client-oriented than would normally be expected of the upper-caste educated. Furthermore, their numbers, together with the general shortage of employment, has made them more accessible and strengthened their clients' bargaining positions. The relationship between lawyers and clients allows the former to introduce new norms to the latter, directly linking them to modern statutes and institutions. In this way, lawyers act as mediators (as opposed to brokers) in three senses: they mediate between traditional and modern legal codes, between center and periphery, and between politicians and bureaucrats.

Their first mediatory function is explained by their familiarity with both traditional customs and modern jurisprudence. Work among villagers has reinforced the lawyers' tendency to be "bi-legal," i.e., to "utilize both indigenous and official law in accordance with their own calculations of propriety and advantage" (Galanter, 1972:64–65). Their second function as middlemen between official centers and the rural periphery is the outcome of their first role. Rephrasing local and provincial interests in terms of official norms, lawyers are vital agents for the expression of these interests at the center of power (Galanter, 1969). In many cases, district-court lawyers, like district-level party functionaries, are strategically located in the political system and link urban and rural sections (Rowe, 1969:221). Third, lawyers often mediate between legal authorities and traditional agents in such matters as marriage, divorce, and inheritance (Rowe, 1969:22).

In sum, the utilization of legal institutions has developed according to two patterns: one differentiated and the other fused or hybrid. Differentiation between ancient and modern law has increased the structural flexibility and efficiency of the legal system but diminished its legitimacy. Fusion of the two has reinforced legitimacy and diminished efficiency (Derrett, 1979). In this sense, one may describe the Indian legal system not only as a blend of "status" and "contract" (see Maine, 1930) but as based on the marriage of three elements: customary codes, legal codes, and politics.[5] The result is quasi-legal and can be interpreted as a system of laws in the making in which no clear boundary has been defined between deviancy and correct behavior. This system is sensitive to the demands of various interests and open to different interpretations. It has provided India with a flexible framework of rules of behavior, which has limited deviancy (although it has not prevented it) and, on the whole, has reduced the possibility of social anomie. A more rigid, one-sided legal system would probably have increased the gap between rules and their implementation and would have encouraged extra-institutional behavior.

THE MUNICIPAL PANCHAYAT SYSTEM

The *panchayat raj* system is a second major "objective" agent which combines legal, administrative, and political codes. It was developed in an attempt to give new meaning and functions to an older institution. The image of the traditional Indian *panchayat,* which has been described as a grass-roots institution, has been idealized by both Indians (e.g., Narayan, 1970) and Britons (e.g., Baden-Powell, *Indian Village Community,* 1896). Its reconstruction has often been described as an attempt to revive the idea of community democracy (Maddick, 1970). Empirically, however, it can best be defined as an agent providing a legal base for the local power structure, accommodating class and primordial interests within "objective" boundaries. In this sense, it seems to function as a mechanism legalizing socio-political differences and/or politicizing legal procedures (rather than differentiating between the two).

Due to the fusion of legal and political spheres, the *panchayat* system is somewhat restricted in terms of policy implementation, although in some parts of India it acts as a planning commission, creating an infrastructure for agricultural and industrial development (thus linking economic and political spheres). Of greater importance to our discussion, however, is the *panchayat*'s several latent functions.

Firstly, the village *panchayat* provides a useful filter for the selection of local leaders. Secondly, it acts to channel the socio-economic demands of the periphery to the center. Thirdly, it is utilized as an avenue for political mobility by local enterpreneurs, so that it can be looked upon as an intermediary institution which converts local into national power. In this way, the *panchayat* contributes to both the unification and the fragmentary character of Indian democracy.

Like India's legal institutions, the village *panchayat* can be viewed as an institutional mechanism based on the blending of traditional customs and modern codes and having judicial and political functions (Bondurant, 1958; Galanter, 1972:58–59; Inamdar, 1970; Maddick, 1970; Mandelbaum, 1970: 278). As such, it was among the most important devices used by the Gandhian movement to mobilize political support (J.M. Brown, 1972:Ch.9).

The modern image of the village *panchayat,* as put forth by Narayan in the 1940s, was of a revival "in all their glory and with their old authority" and their establishment as bodies "exercising revenues, executive and judicial authority" (1970:47). Narayan interpreted the function of the *panchayat* in hybrid terms. He argued that the system must be simplified and modernized so that it "might enable us to combine the best of both the ancient and most modern systems" (1970:47). In fact, the concrete tasks of the *panchayats* were formulated in purely modern terms and stressed economic development. They were supposed to deal with health problems, the development of banking systems, and the abolition of caste boundaries. Political and judicial functions were also formulated in broad modern terms; the aim was to establish a "village republic, not merely [a] panchayat." Following independence the *panchayats* were supported by the Indian Constitution: "The State shall take steps to organize village panchayats and endow them with such powers and authority as may be necessary to enable them to function as units of self-government" (Article 40). In the 1950s the *panchayats* were, to an extent, judicially oriented bodies aimed at reducing the gap between villagers and the legal system. They later became popularly elected semi-political bodies (Galanter, 1972:258–259), which facilitated their spread throughout India (see Table 7:1).

TABLE 7:1

THE GROWTH OF THE PANCHAYAT SYSTEM, 1961–1971

	1961	1971
Number of village *panchayats*	193,527	219,119
Number of *panchayat samities* (block councils)	1,449	3,339
Number of *zilla parishads* (district councils)	133	231
Total number of villages covered by *panchayati raj*	502,337	564,307
Percentage of rural population covered	92	98

Source: Statistical Abstract of the Indian Union, 1972, Table 251, p. 647.

Once *panchayat* members were elected, however, they became official government agents considered above politics and expected to guide the activities of administrative officials. In that sense, the institution has effected a partial shift on the local level from a purely administrative framework to a more politically oriented system. This has prepared the way for the articulation of particularistic interests on the local level among *jati* (caste) associations (Inamdar, 1970). Such a development can be seen as an attempt on the part of ruling groups at the state level to strengthen their position by establishing a foothold in rural areas (Kothari, 1970a:127). At the same time, the system has increased the bargaining position of the rural periphery through local leaders. The *panchayat* has often provided an arena for local politicians who "begin to realize the potentialities of new institutions as a source of power..." and therefore "often prefer positions in Panchayat Samities and Zilla Parishads, and other local institutions to being elected to state legislature" (Kothari, 1970a:136). In this sense, the system can be considered a tool for the dispersion of power.

Another important aspect of the new village *panchayat* system is that it provides an instrument for coping with internal disputes on the village level. Increasing competition between *jatis* due to the erosion of traditional customs has created a need for a new institutional framework able to deal with open conflicts. The village *panchayat* system seems to have fulfilled this role. The policies which it tends to adopt have been based on a synthesis of traditional and modern concepts (Kothari, 1970a:132–135). In an analysis of the distribution of "action programs" on the village level, A. Singh established that out of a total of 77 actions, 40 were in the modern and 37 in the traditional direction (1973:55). Traditional action was defined as conforming to an established way of life handed down from the past, including religious festivals and customs.

The hybrid pattern of the *panchayat* can best be understood by comparing it with modern judicial agents. In the ideal sense, the main differences are three-fold (Mandelbaum, 1970:310–311). First, the *panchayat* considers all the circumstances of a case; the court, for the most part, considers specific circumstances. Second, the *panchayat* considers the entire personalities of the disputants; the court, their relevant traits only. Third, *panchayat* decision-making does not have a formal base; rather, policies and disputes are decided by a process of bargaining and compromise. Since each official largely represents his family or caste, the decision-making process is frequently corrupt and arbitrary. It is, however, precisely these traits that convert the system into a mediatory mechanism, thereby increasing its efficiency in promoting social change.

Beteille (1969:154–155) shows that the *panchayat* system contributed to structural changes in rural areas in three ways: first, because the new *panchayats* are elected bodies, the numerical size of *jatis* is of greater significance than in the past, when primordial status and wealth were the main components of power. Secondly, there is competition even among powerful upper castes as to who will dominate the *panchayat*. Consequently, support from lower castes is sought and their position improved. Thirdly, the locus of power can shift from the caste system itself to a differentiated structure based on functional groups. This means that the *panchayat* is no longer a federation of *jatis* or a body dominated by one caste only, but tends to be gradually transformed into a more universally based, objective institution (Sen et al., 1967).

Like all other bridging institutions, the *panchayat* system could not have been established, even to the limited degree it has functioned, without the leadership of the educated, and their spreading to the periphery (Bendix, 1964). A survey made by the National Institute of Community Development in 1965 of 353 political leaders in 365 villages in sixteen states revealed that about 80 percent of them had received some education. More than half of them had received a secondary education or above, and 13.6 percent had at least matriculated (Arora, 1972:247). While the representation of illiterate leaders in the *panchayat* system has increased in recent years, it is clear that the educated retain central positions. This may be explained by the relatively slight difference in socio-economic status between the educated and the peripheral groups.

The existence of the village *panchayat*, led by local politicians in a corporate pattern, sometimes presents a major obstacle to economic change. The bargaining process among local powers in the *panchayats*, although providing an institutional arena for the resolution of disputes, may retard the process of rational decision-making. In this context, S.N. Dubey (1973) found that when the demand for facilities and services is greater than their supply (a critical dilemma in India), decisions regarding the allocation of facilities tend to be largely governed by irrational factors, that is, in terms of what will mobilize political support (*Seminar,* 1975).

In sum, the *panchayat* system can be seen as an institution which accommodates interests in a semi-formal framework. Socio-economic conflicts are thus channelled and converted into legal and political activities. At the same time, the system enables the dominant classes to legitimize and maintain their position, while its representative structure and legal boundaries somewhat limit their maneuverability. In general, it is the combination of administrative, legal, and judicial codes in both traditional and modern aspects which makes the system so relevant to the problem of integration and legitimacy (Rowe, 1969:233).

THE CIVIL ADMINISTRATION

The bureaucrats of developing countries are subjected to strong cross-pressures. On the one hand, they are guided by Western administrative codes; on the other, they are under the pressure of various particularistic forces and traditional arrangements (Riggs, 1964). Administrators exposed to such cross-pressures may respond in two different ways: they may either debureaucratize their role to make it more flexible, or they may over-bureaucratize it as a defense mechanism, tying themselves to rigid rules and thereby cutting themselves off from their clientele (Eisenstadt, 1965; La Palombara, 1967). The first pattern is most likely to surface when there are more applicants than bureaucratic positions so that administrators are forced to court their clientele. The second pattern is most likely to occur when competition is less acute. In this situation, administrators have a monopoly over their clientele.

The Indian Administrative Service (IAS) has blended strict bureaucratic rules, on the one hand, and political grass-roots, on the other, in an attempt to combine different cultural models into one framework (Dwarkadas, 1958; Heginbotham, 1975; Prasad, 1974; Raghaviah, 1968; Rajon, 1969).

The Indian administration during the colonial period has been described as an efficient machine which, from a formal viewpoint, closely resembled Weber's "ideal type" of bureaucracy (Misra, 1970; Tinker, 1966), while the degree of freedom allowed top level decision-makers, the majority of whom were British, represented the major deviation from this "ideal type" (Lamb, 1968:68; Tinker, 1966). Lower positions were held by Indians, who were less bureaucratically oriented; they maintained a degree of affiliation with the native population and employed traditional methods (N.C. Roy, 1958:313–314). Nevertheless, in terms of principles and prestige, the civil service administration was so far removed from the vast majority of the population that it was for the most part an unlegitimated instrumental tool. "The British administrative system was of a colonial type and while good enough for maintaining law and order, was not suitable for promoting public welfare" (Rajon, 1969:97).

After the 1920s with increased decentralization and political participation of indigenous groups, the administrative machine was adjusted somewhat to the traditional structure and became less bureaucratic. Since independence and the spread of the voting franchise, debureaucratization has been encouraged and supported on the local and state levels, albeit less so on the Union level, which is less influenced by provincial pressures (Potter, 1966).

Debureaucratization has been furthered by a combination of factors. Firstly, candidates for the IAS are not selected on the basis of merit alone but also according to ascriptive affiliations, such as caste, region, and religion. Even the constitutional regulations specify that a certain percentage of the lower classes must be represented in the administration.

Equally important is the fact that heads of offices and departments in the administration are conscious of the problem of primordial representation. It is often in their own interests to adopt an ascriptive policy of recruitment since it enables them to expand their power and influence (Baks, 1976; Jagannadham, 1974; Taub, 1969). The *Report of the Committee on Reservation for Backward Classes in the Services* found that most officials try to implement the policy of reserving places for backward classes without abolishing universalistic criteria, although it is becoming more difficult (1962:13).

Generally speaking, many Indian administrators are not bureaucrats but rather "enlightened" semi-politicians who deploy primordial symbols and affiliations in an administrative setting. They are bound to particularistic obligations, on the one hand, and committed to filling rational official roles, on the other (Baks, 1976; Bansal, 1974:57).

This duality has three major effects. First, it helps them to link the center and periphery. Second, it enables them to mitigate clashes between contradictory interests and orientations (Baks, 1976; Eldersveld et al., 1968; Jagannadham, 1974; Vajpeyi, 1977). Third, it influences the nature of the whole administrative system in several ways: it reduces bureaucratic objectivity and neutrality, making the system less rigid and open to bargaining so that the bureaucracy often approaches a grass-roots type (Tilman, 1963:213ff). Consequently, the Indian bureaucratic system may be defined as combining strict rules and ambiguity (Prasad, 1974:110).

The growth of the IAS in recent years must also be taken into account. Numbering one million employees during the pre-independence period, it grew to two million in 1950, increased more than three-fold to seven million in 1960/61, and reached more than ten million by 1970 (See Table 7:2). This growth has been accompanied by a simultaneous spread to the periphery, which has exposed the service to various particularistic pressures. Administrators have consequently been forced to expand their role and display more flexibility.

TABLE 7:2

GROWTH IN CIVIL ADMINISTRATION EMPLOYEES
(in millions)

	Central Government	State Government	Quasi-Government	Local Bodies	Total
1911	–	–	–	–	0.97*
1931	–	–	–	–	0.99*
1950	–	–	–	–	2.00
1960/61	2.09	3.01	0.77	1.17	7.04
1970/71	2.70	4.10	1.90	1.90	10.60

*Statistics include both India and Pakistan.

Sources: lines 1,2: *Census of India, 1931,* Vol. I, Pt. I, Report Table 4, p. 314; lines 3,4: *Statistical Abstract of the Indian Union, 1965,* Table 134, p. 349; line 5: *Statistical Abstract of the Indian Union, 1972,* Table 136, p. 328.

Weiner (1965:12, 263–264) found that the Indian administration has a more diffuse function than that in the West. Its power over regulatory and distributive functions encompasses services which "help those who cannot otherwise help themselves." With this role extension comes further political involvement: "The party is increasingly called upon to serve as a liaison with the local administration... [and] ...politicians and bureaucrats have in general learned to use each other to achieve their own ends" (Weiner, 1967:51). The very thin line between party "influence" and "interference" (as Weiner refers to it) serves to legitimize administrative activity. Indeed, in some cases, bureaucrats assume semi-autonomous political and cultural roles which are not clearly associated with national political parties.

Taub (1969) and Baks (1976) have reported a strong tendency among administrators to work in the districts in order to gain more satisfaction and power. In fact, local administrative newcomers have little choice but to assume peripheral positions to overcome a sense of abstraction in dealing with problems; they also prefer to deal directly with their clients rather than to be subject to the supervision of politicians. However, those who cannot adjust to the dual pressures develop a pattern of behavior characterized "by inflexible adherence to and dependence upon rules.... This generalized rigidity prevents the organization from adapting readily to changing demands upon it" (Taub, 1969:60). Indian civil servants, especially those belonging to the higher echelons, have been described as generalists rather than specialists, making them more successful in politics than in the economic and technical spheres. This has enabled them to extend their role and to aggregate more power than is permitted by law (Bhambhri, 1971:266–267).

The political involvement of administrators reinforces the bureaucracy's grass-roots connections, making the whole system flexible and more relevant to society in the sense that it nurtures personal relationships between clients and civil servants. In this context, Indian administrators can be perceived as social mediators attempting to connect the "old" and "new" orders (N.C. Roy, 1958:14; Vepa, 1967:228–229).

In his discussion of the Indian bureaucracy, Potter (1966:208) notes that the IAS has contributed to political stability with respect to the maintenance of internal peace, administration of fair elections, and preservation of the unity of the nation. In the economic sphere it has also been active in initiating public enterprises and rural development. He concludes that changing the political behavior of government officials, in terms of bureaucratic responsibility, would result in less effective performance with regard to economic policy.

These diffuse roles and relationships, existing under conditions of duality, lead to the infiltration of various forms of corruption. The Santhanam Committee summed up the issue:

> There is a general impression that it is difficult to get things done without resorting to corruption. Scope for corruption is greater and the incentive to corrupt stronger at those points of the organization where substantive decisions are taken in matters like assessment and collection of taxes, determination of eligibility for obtaining license, grant of licenses, ensuring fair utilization of licenses and goods obtained thereunder, giving of contracts, approval of works and acceptance of supplies... in all contracts of construction, purchases, sales and other regular business on behalf of the government, a regular percentage is paid by the parties to the transaction, and this is shared in agreed proportions among the various officials concerned (quoted by Bhambhri, 1971:268).

Corruption has been conventionally defined as a special type of deviance in which actors use their position according to unacceptable standards (Alatas, 1968; Scott, 1969). A complementary point of view sees corruption as a special type of transaction between public officials and their clients in which the amount and/or kind of commodities under exchange are not legitimized. Smelser (1971) defines corruption as "a particular kind of crossing over of economic and political rewards" in which wealth, power, influence, and value commitments are exchanged in an undifferentiated way.

The rules of exchange are a combination of codes based on "status" and "contract" principles. The development of this diffuse and undifferentiated pattern of exchange is explained by the Indian conditions of duality. Under these conditions, the normative boundaries are not clear and there are many options of behavior. It is least costly to find a middle road, combining traditional and modern rules, where any type of behavior may be perceived as corrupt from at least one standpoint. In general, it seems that corruption can be perceived as a social mechanism by which public officials in developing countries mediate between traditional and modern codes.

In India the present legal standards "offer the civil servant or politician much less scope for manoeuvre than his counterpart in Europe a century ago" (Scott, 1969:318). However, these standards cannot be applied rigidly without some modifications which combine different rules. Receiving gifts from clients or allocating benefits and positions to relatives is accepted as legitimate behavior by large sectors of the traditional population, although this kind of behavior is defined as corrupt according to official codes (Monterio, 1966:Ch. 1). Thus, many Indian officials (in the police force, courts, and administration) must act "corruptly" in order to gain traditional legitimation of their roles. The efficiency of public agencies often depends on their ability to be "corrupted," that is, to adjust to customary laws.

The most common types of corruption are illegitimate profiteering and bribery (Halayya, 1975; Kolhi, 1975; Monterio, 1966; Taub, 1969:39ff). The latter helps the bureaucrat determine the priorities of resource allocation (Taub, 1969:142–144). In both cases the political and economic spheres become fused, and antagonism between them may be reduced. In his *Burmese Days*, George Orwell gave the impression that the use of various methods that were corrupt from a legal standpoint rarely prevented the proper functioning of the legal system: "His practice was to take a bribe from both sides and then to decide the case on strictly legal grounds" (1963:8).

Another example of corruption is the exchange of power and influence. Officials generally favor people from their own primordial group; they purchase status and affiliation by the use of power. Another common phenomenon is the utilization of government property for private purposes. This is not merely a *zamindari* or feudal pattern, as described by Taub (1969:148); rather, it is mainly a transaction whereby an individual tries to fuse public and private interests. The loyalty of an official to his job may even increase in this way.

In general, in societies where a dual structure exists, it is almost impossible to define exact rules of behavior; double standards exist and widespread "corrupt" methods are to be anticipated. In the case of India it seems worthwhile to examine the extent to which the system has developed tools for controlling corruption and reducing arbitrariness in the settling of disputes and in policy-making. The fact that there are several bridging mechanisms, as mentioned above, increases the ability of the system to cope with arbitrariness because what has been dealt with in a "corrupt" way by one mechanism is sometimes curbed by another.

On the whole the three "objective" mechanisms have been used interchangeably to cope with problems. It is this flexibility as well as the internal hybrid structure of each institution which explains their mediatory power.

There is one other "objective" mechanism which should be considered in terms of its mediatory potential. We refer to the mass media.

THE MASS MEDIA

While the mass media have often been regarded as an instrument for the promotion of national integration, they can as easily serve a disintegrative function, segregating groups and sectors.

The function of the media in a given society generally depends upon social conditions. We are concerned with the degree to which the mass media serve as intermediary mechanisms or, more specifically, the extent to which they act as independent agents linking different values and groups. In that respect, a mediatory mass medium is not a mere instrument of transmission but rather a translative or reinterpretive mechanism which can bridge antagonisms regardless of whether messages are consumed directly through the media or passed on via public opinion leaders and social networks. Keeping this definition in mind, we will consider the extent to which the Indian mass media fill a mediatory role.

Firstly, while the network of mass media may be considered "objective" in the sense that it is expected to be operated according to a semi-professional ethic and "the public interest," actual circumstances indicate that such an ethic can only partially be realized in India. Secondly, the efficiency of the system is weakened by the absence of an absorptive infrastructure in much of India's countryside, widespread illiteracy, and a limited audience. Thirdly, as in the majority of developing societies, efficiency of communication depends on the pattern and degree to which the mass media are linked to traditional grass-roots networks. The decline of the traditional networks of communication without a corresponding emergence of substitute patterns has had a disintegrative effect. Traditional networks (generally primordial social networks, which transmit orally), especially prominent in rural India, may have found it difficult to absorb modern messages without undergoing transformation.

Fourthly, and perhaps most importantly, mass media in India can be considered a uni-directional transmittory mechanism (center to periphery), unable to represent particularistic interests. This one-sidedness has been described by journalists themselves:

> The right to be heard is as necessary, especially in a country where the 'have nots' abound, as the right to communicate. Without it, communication becomes a barren one-way traffic.... At present, the right to be

heard is available only to those who are ready to wrest it and hold it (Jain, 1979:12–13).

Furthermore, media messages are too numerous and relatively sophisticated to be grasped and utilized by a population with a thirty percent literacy rate and a low level of modern education.

It should also be noted that all forms of broadcasting are controlled by the federal government. All India Radio (AIR) broadcasts government policies among other items and, according to its code, may *not* broadcast "...attacks on religions or communities..., attacks on political parties by name, or hostile criticism of any state or the center" (Awasthy, 1978:204). Further, it "has the right to censor, edit, or amend the text" of any sponsored show aired on its stations. Television, still in its infancy, is also under government auspices (M.V. Desai, 1977).

Due to the lack of sufficient research on the subject, our analysis is necessarily incomplete. However, it seems that most of the mass media are not dual, exhaustive, or reciprocal, all of which are necessary characteristics of a mediatory mechanism. Only the press has maintained a relatively independent structure and therefore may carry enough mediatory power to warrant discussion.

The press in India is primarily a means of communication among educated elites. Although there were 821 dailies out of a total of about twelve thousand newspapers in 1971, total circulation did not exceed 3.6 million (see Table 7:3). Papers are published in sixty languages and can be read by most local leaders. About sixty-two percent are privately owned. Political parties also own papers: the Congress Party has thirty-five newspapers, the two Communist parties have thirty-one, and the other parties have two to five newspapers each (*Press in India*, 1972).

TABLE 7:3

GROWTH IN NEWSPAPERS AND PERIODICALS
1966–1971

	Number		Circulation (in thousands)	
	1966	1971	1966	1971
Dailies	549	821	616	943
Weeklies	2,455	2,676	516	539
Others	5,636	7,721	2,222	2,185
Total	8,640	12,218	3,554	3,667

Source: Press in India, 1972, Pt. 1, Table 1, p. 17, Table 214, p. 316.

Most Indians have never read a newspaper. According to the *Report of the Press Commission* in 1954, "less than 5 percent of all households surveyed in the rural areas took in newspapers and in about 60 percent of the 'rural blocks' there was not even a single household which read a daily newspaper" (pp. 19–20). However, information published in the newspapers is generally diffused orally to about 60 percent of the total population.

To some extent, newspapers are a tool by which elites compete amongst themselves rather than an instrument for the mobilization of popular support. However, local elites do take advantage of the large number of newspapers published in indigenous languages to select and orally diffuse information to the illiterate majority in the periphery and thereby to gain their support. This pattern of "two steps of communication" has increased the political awareness of the peripheral echelons in Indian society (Banerjee, 1968; P. Narain, 1970; Rangaswami Iyengar, 1933; C. Sarkar, 1967).

Because of the size of the Indian university population there is sufficient qualified manpower to maintain a comparatively large professional press. Professional ethics have developed, and the press has been maintained as an independent "third party" or "fourth estate." It has increased the political fluidity of the elites by diffusing new ideas among them and has also provided an extra-constitutional tool for raising problems, especially for leaders of opposition parties and groups.[6]

With regard to the content of daily newspapers, the *Report of the Press Commission* indicates that many are politically oriented and print editorials aimed at influencing public policy (1954:258–259). However, the press cannot be said to have mass appeal and can hardly be considered a popular mediatory mechanism (P. Narain, 1970:294).[7] Prior to independence the press was mainly a tool for mobilizing the elites against the British (Natarajan, 1962); afterwards it gradually became more oriented toward issues raised by the opposition. It also often lacked efficient tools for collecting information and was occasionally unreliable. The government has often accused the press of spreading rumors and unsubstantiated information (Mankekar, 1973).

In general, the press has filled a limited mediatory function because of its restricted circulation. Nevertheless, it provides a public instrument for maintaining competition among elites,[8] supports the openness of the political structure, and contributes to the elites' sensitivity to various peripheral problems. In this sense, the press can be considered an independent bridging mechanism.

CONCLUSIONS

Our discussion of intermediary institutions in the present and preceding chapter has revealed that they are usually implemented by ruling classes and elites interested in maintaining their dominancy in the system. Such institutions also enable a more egalitarian distribution of rights, power, and resources since they link structural contradictions and codes, thereby providing multiple options in open frameworks for bargaining.

The intermediary mechanisms discussed have contributed to the emergence of a special social order in India in a number of ways. They have increased political participation, produced a social context for institutionalized political competition, and contributed to the conversion of traditional primordial units into universal national ones. Furthermore, the mixed natures of such mechanisms has contributed to the diffusion of modern models of behavior in many echelons of society, the creation of a more common, legitimate culture, and the development of a corporate pluralistic pattern of integration. Equally important, interlinking mechanisms have sometimes provided institutional channels of expression for elites and the periphery alike, thereby reducing the probability that extra-institutional methods will be used. While increasing integration and smoothing the transition from one pattern of order to another, these mediatory mechanisms have also lowered the rate of structural economic change (see Ch. 3). The emergence of fluid voting power and sophisticated political, legal, and administrative institutions (Dasgupta and Morris-Jones, 1976), without the development of parallel economic institutions and fluid manpower, widens divergencies and, in the long run, increasingly endangers the stability of the Indian social order. The declaration of the State of Emergency in 1975 can perhaps be regarded as a response to this danger.

NOTES

1. For a general discussion of the sociology of law, see Gulliver, 1973; Johnson, 1977; Selznick, 1969.

2. For approaches supporting such a definition, see Griffith, 1977; Nonet and Selznick, 1978; Seidman, 1972.

3. For the laws of the Manu, see Muller, 1966.

4. It seems that British contractual law more or less broke the monopoly of the privileged class as the sole articulator of traditional law from the end of the nineteenth century (Maine, 1930: Ch. I). On the other hand, British legality was applied, in a differential way, to different groups and sectors, as is clear from the following quotations:

If we survey the whole field of law, as administered by the British Indian courts, and examine the extent to which it consists of English and of native law respectively, we shall find that Warren Hastings' famous rule, though not binding on the Indian legislatures, still indicates the class of subjects with which the Indian legislatures have been chary of interfering, and which they have been disposed to leave to the domain of native law and usage.

The criminal law and the law of civil and criminal procedure are based wholly on English principles. So also, subject to some few exceptions, are the law of contract and the law of torts, or civil wrongs.

But within the domain of family law, including the greater part of the law of succession and inheritance, natives still retain their personal law, either modified or formulated, to some extent, by Anglo-Indian legislation. Hindus retain their law of marriage, of adoption, of the joint family, of partition, of succession. Mahomedans retain their law of marriage, of testamentary and intestate succession, and of *wakf* or quasi-religious trusts. The important branch of law relating to the tenure of land, as embodied in the Rent and Revenue Acts and regulations of the different provinces, though based on Indian customs, exhibits a struggle and compromise between English and Indian principles.

It will have been seen that the East India Company began by attempting to govern natives by native law, Englishmen by English law. This is the natural system to apply in a conquered country, or in a vassal State – that is to say, a State where complete sovereignty has not been assumed by the dominant power. It is the system which involves the least disturbance (Ilbert, 1898:401).

The implementation of legal rules was dependent on this adaptation to local conditions:

> In India it became necessary to draw up for the guidance of untrained judges and magistrates a set of rules which they could easily understand, and which were adapted to the circumstances of the country. There has been a tendency, on the one hand, to overpraise the formal merits of the Indian codes, and on the other to under-rate their practical utility as instruments of government. Their workmanship, judged by European standards, is often rough, but they are on the whole well adapted to the conditions which they were intended to meet (Ilbert, 1898:404).

5. The effect of Western legislation on various spheres has been differential. The institution of marriage, dowries, and primordial relationships have been less influenced than untouchability and inheritance methods. This differential implementation of law has often increased structural divergence (Derrett, 1979). On the other hand,

> [t]he displacement of indigenous law from the official legal system does not mean the demise of traditional norms and concerns... ...both official courts and indigenous tribunals may be used for a variety of purposes. Official law can be used not only to evade traditional restrictions, but to enforce them. Report to official courts can be had in order to disrupt a traditional panchayat, or to stimulate it into action.... Caste tribunals may be used to promote changes. ...many elements of official law [have been assimilated] into the workings of the indigenous tribunals.... Srinivas' studies indicate that even in villages where there is little recourse to government courts, the form of dispute within the panchayat seems affected by official models in drafting of documents, keeping of records, terminology and procedure (Galanter, 1972:64–65).

See also Ishwaran, 1964; Srinivas, 1969.

6. A good example of this is the Bengali newspaper, The *Bangabashi*, established in 1881; see Banerjee, 1968; Natarajan, 1962.

7. The Press Commission of 1954 found that more than fifty percent of the newspapers were concentrated in the big cities (*Report of the Press Commission*, 1954:44).

8. It is interesting to note that, while the press has been used primarily as a tool for communication among elites in India, it was utilized as a bridging mechanism between the center and periphery in Japan during the restoration (Altman, 1975).

Chapter 8

THE LIMITS OF BRIDGING MECHANISMS:
THE POLITICAL PENDULUM, JUNE 1975 TO MARCH 1977

INTRODUCTION

In his wide-ranging comparative study, Moore argues that: "India belongs to two worlds.... Economically it remains in the pre-industrial age.... But as a political species it does belong to the modern world" (1966:314). In other words, there is divergence between political and economic spheres. Moore suggests three ways in which the gap might be closed. First, the disparity "...could in time perhaps generate its own antithesis, though the difficulties of a radical takeover in India are enormous." A second way would be to allow the upper strata to control the system by utilizing the market mechanism. The third possibility would be to introduce a stronger coercive element, more or less based on the Communist model. Moore concludes, "a strong element of coercion remains necessary if a change is to be made" (1966:409–410).

We have suggested another solution: the bridging of divergence through mediatory institutions. These mechanisms have institutionalized political fluidity while balancing economic development. However, precisely because they mediate between contradictions, they serve to slow down social change. Consequently, redistribution of power has not been paralleled by a redistribution of wealth. With the widening gap, the mediatory institutions have not been strong enough to bridge the divergence.

It is our thesis that the declaration of a State of Emergency in June 1975 represented an attempt to lessen the structural divergence. In other words, there was an attempt to diminish political fluidity and to accelerate the rate of economic change, under the assumption that a shift toward economic development would not be politically risky at a certain level of social integration.

A few preliminary remarks are in order regarding what led India into the State of Emergency and what brought it back to democracy. They concern not so much the immediate events as the extended structural process from which the situations derive. Three issues will be briefly investigated: the extent to which the State of Emergency changed the basic institutional structure of the Indian regime, the social causes of the Emergency, and the factors underlying the March 1977 shifts.

INSTITUTIONAL CHANGE RESULTING FROM THE STATE OF EMERGENCY

The State of Emergency was declared by Prime Minister Indira Gandhi on June 26, 1975, in reaction to a "grave emergency threatened by internal disturbances." The presidential order suspended three key constitutional articles: the guarantee of equal protection for all before the law, protection of life and personal liberty, and protection against unwarranted arrest and detention. During the first three months about 50,000 persons were reportedly arrested and press censorship was imposed. These arrested included certain leaders of the opposition parties of the extreme right (e.g., Jan Sangh); leaders of the pro-China Communist Party, CPI(M); distinguished opponents of corruption, J. Narayan and M. Desai (leader of the "old" Congress Party); members of the ruling Congress Party who were critical of the government; and journalists and editors of leading newspapers. Members of the pro-Moscow Communist Party, CPI, were not arrested.

The State of Emergency can be defined as the end result of a long-term process, characterized by six distinctive developments: (1) a new balance was established among legislative, judicial, and executive powers in favor of the latter; (2) the power of the opposition was severely limited and extreme political groups banned, although some degree of freedom was permitted within narrow boundaries under governmental control; (3) leading politicians and journalists on both the Union and state levels were imprisoned, but the local echelons of politicians at the district and village level were left untouched; (4) strict control over mass communication was imposed; (5) the legislative bodies were forced to rubber stamp constitutional changes to increase the Prime Minister's power; and (6) central control was imposed on state governments and local bodies.

The State of Emergency was a dramatic change in the direction of a more personal and monistic, and less pluralistic, governmental approach. Changes were formally brought about through institutional means and without the destruction of the Indian constitutional infrastructure. At the operational level the basic institutional structure remained steady, although the balance among the several social forces changed. Some of the basic codes of "checks and balances" and of competitive politics remained in the system, but their scope was reduced.

SOCIO-ECONOMIC FACTORS LEADING TO THE STATE OF EMERGENCY

The State of Emergency can be explained by a combination of several major factors which increased structural divergence. As pointed out in Chapter 3, actual economic development in India was modest in comparison with the growth of aspirations. Further, there was only minor redistribution of income (in terms of annual consumer expenditure) among the different echelons of society and between the urban and rural sectors, and little structural change (V.K.R.V. Rao, 1979). These economic conditions, however, did not produce widespread unrest; at least there is no real indication that they posed an immediate threat to the regime. But economic retardation has an aggregate affect. It makes questionable the legitimacy of the political framework (Kothari, 1975, 1976). In the long run, the government could not ignore the accumulated frustrations which were the product of the economic setup.

In the political sphere there was a sharp increase in factionalism (Rastogi, 1975), both within and without the existing party system. Moreover, the various *jati* associations and factions became increasingly fluid. Many were small, loosely organized, and often of a temporary character, which made them able to represent only a narrow range of particularistic interests. In addition, competition among factions encouraged the emergence of more extreme groups, which demanded their share of the national pie but did not acknowledge the society's collective needs. These developments encouraged political diversification and made the implementation of any government policy difficult. Any decision taken was based mainly on a "statistical average" of social forces. Many attempts to implement programs or policies failed due to pressures exerted by groups that would not stand to gain immediate benefits. Under these conditions Mrs. Gandhi's government was often almost paralyzed. This process encouraged the tendency, by both the ruling Congress Party and the opposition, to adopt extra-institutional tactics and thereby further undermine legitimate institutions.

These developments were partially due to the rapid, uncontrolled increase of politically involved educated groups in the population. The rapidly expanded production of students of higher education from the beginning of the century encouraged the spread of educated mediators into the periphery. This process produced more grass-roots politics than was to be expected in a country such as India, but, as the number of educated increased, it also fostered parochial sentiments and organizations. As long as the number of educated did not pass a certain point, their absorption into intermediate institutions was an important political factor.

In the pre-independence period, and perhaps during the following decade, the surplus of educated provided India with the middlemen who established Indian democracy and its pluralistic pattern of integration. Accelerated production of educated from the 1970s and the accompanying unemployment created a large intellectual proletariat.[1] The result was exaggeratedly factional mass politics. While the competitive structure of Indian politics had been an important mechanism in the mitigation of conflicts, the greater number of small pressure groups made competition amorphic. The power of intermediary institutions was thereby significantly diminished (Prasad, 1974). Mass violence and instability resulted.

The State of Emergency aimed to counter these tendencies by controlling political fluidity while simultaneously fostering economic development. The Prime Minister's Twenty Points Program, announced on July 1, 1975, and manifestly accepted widely, was an attempt to shift the emphasis from political integration to a more instrumental, economic-oriented policy. The program had four principal aims: firstly, the encouragement of "productive forces" in the industrial structure, including large capitalist enterprises; secondly, greater efforts to bring about structural changes in the rural areas, including the abolition of landlordism and bonded labor, legislation concerning moratoriums and the recovery of private debts, and increased minimum wages for agricultural workers; thirdly, compensation of the middle classes and the educated through the institution of price controls, increased tax exemptions, and the provision of new employment channels; and, fourthly, strengthening of the administration's implementative capacity through new measures against corruption and the reorganization of district administration.

The program was not new, but the State of Emergency provided the structural conditions for its implementation. What is important is that the Indian social system was able to absorb the impact of these measures without losing its basic institutional character. However, in the long run, a structural contradiction exists between the pluralistic nature of Indian society and the trend to develop a more monistic (or autocratic) pattern of government. Attempts to restrict the institutional channels of expression of various particularistic interests may invite more extra-institutional activities.

The choice faced by Mrs. Gandhi's government was between reduced political competition and increased implementative power in the economic sphere, on the one hand, and maintenance of a competitive political structure and less economic progress, on the other. The former would gain it more ad hoc support, but threaten political legitimacy. The latter course could consolidate the legitimacy of the ruling center but accelerate economic deterioration. The ruling center seemed to have decided to sacrifice some degree of political legitimacy in order to promote economic development. Under these circumstances any economic failure would be likely to threaten the entire system.

THE 1977 ELECTIONS AND THE END OF THE STATE OF EMERGENCY

After approximately eighteen months of the Emergency, general elections were held in the middle of March 1977. Despite the fact that the country was almost fully controlled by Mrs. Gandhi's government and the ruling Congress Party, both the Prime Minister in her own constituency and the Congress Party were defeated. The elections brought to power a new group, the Janata Party, composed of four smaller parties. Of 542 seats in the Lok Sabha, the Congress Party secured only 153, while the Janata Party gained 271 (see Table 8:1). The new government, with M. Desai as its Prime Minister, was made up of a coalition of the Janata Party and the Congress of Democracy (CFD), the latter led by the former Minister of Agriculture, Mr. Ram.

TABLE 8 : 1

DISTRIBUTION OF LOK SABHA SEATS
BEFORE AND AFTER THE MARCH 1977 ELECTIONS

	Fifth L.S. Jan. 1977		Sixth L.S. March 1977
Congress (New)	355		153
CPI (Communists)	24		7
CPI (Marxists)	26		22
Unattached	28	(CFD)	28
ADMK	6		19
Socialists	3		
BLD	9	(Janata Party)	271
Jan Sangh	16		
Congress (Old)	11		
UIPG	8		–
DMK	12		1
Others	9		31
Independents	–		8
Vacant	17		2*
Total Seats	524		539

*Polling for two seats was not completed in March 1977.

Source: Overseas Hindustan Times, March 31 and April 7, 1977.

This political shift ended the State of Emergency, a fact which became clear when, after the election and before its exit from office, the old government suggested to Acting President B.D. Jatti that the State of Emergency be revoked. As a follow-up, several notifications were issued by the Union Home Ministry, including one to restore the "seven freedoms" that had been suspended during the Emergency. The most important of these basic freedoms was the right of any person to apply to the court for the enforcement of the fundamental rights conferred by Articles 14, 21, and 22 of the Constitution and for habeas corpus.

Another notification allowed for the release of all political prisoners and detainees under the Maintenance of Internal Security Act (MISA) and the Conservation of Foreign Exchange and Prevention of Smuggling Act (COFEPOSA), except for those against whom firm grounds of detention had been made or whose detention had been ordered by the courts. In addition, the ban imposed on twenty-six organizations, including the Rashtriya Swayamasevak Sangh (RSS), Jamaat-e-Islamic Hind, and Anand Marg, was lifted, and their members were released from detention.

Following its establishment the new government declared its most urgent task to be the removal of the remaining curbs on fundamental freedoms and civil rights, as well as the restoration of the rule of law and the right of free expression to the press. It was faced with certain constitutional difficulties in revoking Emergency amendments, but eventually managed to overcome them.

What were the events that led up to the 1977 elections and the Janata Party victory? These may be divided into two types: those motivated by the Congress Party to ensure re-election and those that eventually shook the foundations of the ruling party.

With regard to the former, three steps were taken by Mrs. Gandhi in an attempt to assure both an easy victory and relegitimation of the regime. First, her government nearly paralyzed the opposition through constitutional and extra-constitutional means. Second, the holding of elections in March 1977 was declared on short notice (on January 18, 1977). Third, Mrs. Gandhi withdrew some of the Emergency measures and released certain opposition leaders from prison shortly before election day.

Two other pre-election events seemed to weaken the position of the current regime: the merger of some of the major opposition parties into the Janata Party and the resignation of the influential Mr. Ram, Minister of Agriculture. While these changes were not perceived as a threat by Mrs. Gandhi and the Congress Party at the beginning of the election campaign, a few weeks later it became clear that a deeply motivated protest movement was underlying the Janata Party's strength. This movement contained parts of the less established elites that had not enjoyed the benefits of the regime; some of the business classes, protesting government corruption and nepotism; and peasants and urban lower classes, especially of northern India, protesting harsh methods of policy implementation, particularly compulsory sterilization as part of governmentally controlled family planning. These seeds of protest were then catalyzed and crystallized into political voting power by the leadership of three old comrades of Mahatma Gandhi: M. Desai, J.P. Narayan, and J.B. Kripalani. These men were able to unite different political forces and to increase the consensus within opposing factions.

Structurally speaking, the victory of the Janata Party may be attributed, first of all, to Mrs. Gandhi's inability to act rapidly in the economic sphere. She had made an effort to gain credit by accelerating economic growth and had achieved some success in this venture. However, the shift toward emphasis on economic goals was made at the expense of social integration, as exemplified by changes in tax policy. The government sharply lowered the rates of income and wealth taxes between the years 1974/75 and 1976/77 from a maximum income tax rate of 97.75 percent to one of 60 percent. The wealth tax was reduced from 8 percent to 2.5 percent (*Economic and Political Weekly*, XII, April 5, 1977:583). The policy aimed at increasing economic activity among the wealthier classes and at raising the national income. However, the economic benefits of the policy were too slight to win support for the regime but strong enough to produce a disintegrative effect.

Politically, the situation was more complicated. The legitimacy of the regime had been considerably shaken by steps taken to paralyze the opposition and censor the press, measures which left little institutional space for protest to factions and counter-elites. An important indicator of the decrease in legitimacy was the widespread use of police force.[2] The 1977 elections can be perceived as Mrs. Gandhi's attempt to relegitimize her regime by using the "old" competitive institutional structure. Her defeat certainly showed that the institutional arrangements in India have been sufficiently flexible to adjust to changing conditions.

The most important institutional change in 1977 was the establishment of the Janata Party. This was perhaps a major attempt to decrease political factionalism without diminishing competition and fluidity. The party was created by the merger of the Jan Sangh, Old Congress Party, Bharatya Lok Dal (BLD) and Socialists. The largest component was the Jan Sangh, which has been labelled a militant Hindu party. The Socialist Party stands at the opposite end of the political spectrum. In between these two poles, the Old Congress Party and the BLD represent a more moderate approach. The unification of these streams was difficult and only partially successful.

In general, the State of Emergency and the 1977 elections can both be perceived as attempts to increase the convergence of political institutions and economic development, differing only with regard to means. While Mrs. Gandhi reduced the fluidity of politics by its regimentation, the Janata Party attempted to do this by unifying political powers in a quasi-democratic way. This made politics even more fluid and thereby increased divergence within the economic sphere. Consequently, factional politics was encouraged and decision-making became more difficult.

The general elections of January 1980 saw the reinstatement of Mrs. Gandhi and the Congress Party. Their victory can be viewed as a consequence of the Janata Party's inability to manipulate fluid politics. It seems this changeover was accompanied by the adoption of a middle-of-the-road policy between open and closed politics.

Despite the changes in power and policy implementation, the "grammar" of Indian politics did not undergo any crucial transformation during the Emergency or after the elections of 1977 and 1980; factional organizations remained the best tool to gain economic benefits.

CONCLUSIONS

One of the most prominent characteristics of Indian society has been the growing divergence between political and economic institutions. While political institutions have become more fluid, a large number of economic institutions have retained their traditional rigidity. The Indian social system has mitigated this divergence by utilizing various mediatory mechanisms (see Chs. 6 and 7). The operators of the system, the educated elite, have been able to mobilize power although they have lacked the necessary economic resources to implement policy. The surplus of political goods (i.e., power) and the lack of economic goods in the hands of the active members of society have encouraged exchange between the two spheres. This exchange has contributed to the intermixture of contradictory societal codes, which in turn has increased corruption and reduced the system's capacity to cope with its problems.

In most developing countries the establishment of an autocratic government (military or civil) can be perceived as an attempt to increase the convergence of political and economic institutions by reducing the fluidity of the former and developing the latter. The capacity of an autocratic government to promote a market-oriented economy, however, is doubtful (McKinlay and Cohan, 1975). Any economic development promotes fluid groups pressing for participation in the decision-making process, which then becomes a threat to an authoritative regime.

There are two other alternative solutions to the problem of divergence. One is to establish intermediary institutions like those in India. This, however, has a limited effect above certain thresholds of institutional divergence. The other is to adopt laissez faire methods based on interest representation. However, under conditions of social divisiveness and economic scarcity this solution accentuates contradictions without providing mechanisms for coping with them.

NOTES

1. The major sources on unemployment in India are *Report of the Committee of Experts on Unemployment Estimates,* 1970, and *Report of the Committee on Unemployment,* 1973.

As indicated in the table below, the number of colleges in India increased from 849 to 2,099 between 1950/51 and 1960/61 and the number of students, from 403,519 to over a million. In the following decade the former increased to 3,604 and the latter to more than three million. Between 1911/12 and 1970/71 the number of colleges increased almost twenty-fold, and the number of students more than eighty-fold.

Development of Indian Higher Education
1911–1971

	Number of Colleges	Growth Index	Rate of Growth per Decade	Number of Students	Growth Index	Rate of Growth per Decade
1911/12*	186	100		36,000	100	
1920/21*	228	123	1.22	61,324	170	1.70
1930/31*	317	170	1.30	92,028	225	1.50
1940/41*	410	220	1.20	152,962	424	1.66
1950/51	849	456	2.07	403,519	1,120	2.63
1960/61	2,099	1,128	2.47	1,034,930	2,875	2.56
1970/71	3,604	1,938	1.71	3,001,792	8,337	2.89

* The data for 1911/12 and 1920/21 include Burma; for those years, plus 1930/31 and 1940/41, they include Pakistan as well.

Data computed from: lines 1,2: *Statistical Abstract for British India, 1911/12–1920/21,* Table 151, p. 299, Table 144, p. 286; line 3: *Statistical Abstract for British India, 1930/31,* Table 137, p. 368; line 4: *Statistical Abstract of the Indian Union, 1949,* Table 32, p. 120; line 5: *Statistical Abstract of the Indian Union, 1951/52,* Table 28, p. 75; lines 6,7: *University Grants Commission: Report for the Year 1970/71,* Appendix III, p. 43.

2. For example, the total expenditure of the police force was increased from Rs 329 crores in 1970/71 to Rs 689 crores in 1976/77 (*Economic and Political Weekly,* XII, April 9, 1977:584).

Chapter 9

EPILOGUE: INDIAN DEMOCRACY ON TRIAL

INTRODUCTION

In this chapter we shall attempt to illustrate how the approach in this book applies to the current situation in India, as well as its usefulness in comparative studies of other societies. Our thesis is that Indian society has been able to create stable social change because continued trends of increasing antagonism have been accompanied by changing patterns in mediatory mechanisms.

To avoid speculation we analyze the current Indian case in terms of the theoretical categories and indicators utilized earlier in this book. The first part of this chapter describes the changing patterns of antagonism; the second is devoted to the changing nature of several mediatory mechanisms; and the final section offers a few general conclusions.

CHANGING PATTERNS OF ANTAGONISM

We have argued throughout this book that antagonism has been accentuated in India. In recent years the pattern of conflicts has changed in that they have become more violent and are now characterized by the increasing use of non-institutional means. This change can be illustrated by: various conflicts rooted in class differences; violence against the harijans in the rural areas; and the riots between outside laborers and the local population as a result of inland migration.

Indian society is essentially rural in nature; in 1981 about 76 percent of the population lived in villages (Visaria and Visaria, 1981:1751). Most Indians earn their livelihood from agricultural work, using simple, traditional farming methods. Social changes over the last hundred or so years have nevertheless succeeded in raising the level of rural aspirations so significantly that it now resembles that of the middle classes. The resulting gap between reality and expectations has accentuated the sense of deprivation among the lower village classes. Strains among rural groups have been aggravated as a result of the limited employment opportunities both within and without the village. In addition, differential development, whereby some sectors and groups have substantially improved their position while others stood still, has widened the gap between castes, between lower- and middle-class peasants, and, within the middle class, between the cultivators or businessmen and the salaried groups (V.M. Rao, 1981:1661–1662). There has also been an increase in the free-floating proletariat. Consequently, the conflict within the villages has become more open and violent.

As illustrated in the case of Tamil Nadu, where the Naxalite movement has taken the law into its own hands, intra-village conflicts also interact with national politics:

> The tiny village of Kadirampatti in Tirupattur taluk is a classic example of the conditions that have helped the resurgence of Naxalite activity. Here 170 caste Hindu families have kept 300 Harijan families in virtual bondage. Even today the Harijans dare not walk the streets of Kadi-rampatti wearing a white dhoti or with chappals. As against the minimum prescribed wage of Rs 7 for a farm worker (Rs 5 for women), the practice in this village is to engage Harijan for an annual payment of Rs 350 and two meals a day. The "take home" wage is less than even this paltry sum, as part of the wages are paid as advance and the rest is calculated as interest on the sum advanced. When the Harijans resorted to crop cutting as a part of their strategy to get justice, the landlords, with the help of the civil authorities organised "self-protection" committees.
>
> Legislations like debt relief have remained only on paper. Bonded labour is widely prevalent and indebted farm workers even pledge their teenaged sons and daughters with the landlords. Untouchability is still practised in a primitive form (Correspondent, Tamil Nadu, "Myths and Facts Behind Agrarian Unrest," *Economic and Political Weekly*, XVI, December 1981:2027).

Under conditions such as those the lower classes and castes have no choice but to develop extra-institutional means to improve their position.

Boundaries between *jatis* and castes have become more flexible due to the increased "openness" of the Indian village, the significant rise in free-floating manpower, a diminishing belief in transmigration of the soul, and the vanishing practice of segregating rituals. In consequence, clashes between castes have been accentuated (D. Gupta, 1981). The increased primordial strain is often expressed by violent action, particularly against the relatively defenseless harijans.

Several events reported in the newspapers seem to suggest that upper-caste groups have been exploiting caste strains to massacre harijans and thereby promote their own interests. As the individual harijans lack the power to defend themselves, they receive little protection from the police and other institutionalized bodies. They have therefore begun to step up collective self-defense, under the autonomous leadership of militants drawn from their own ranks, a process which began in the 1930s (Henningham, 1981:1153), but has recently become more widespread (Joshi, 1981:1361).

Unrest has also grown as a result of the continuous internal migration from the underdeveloped to developing areas of India caused by differential economic development. This has led to frequent clashes between native residents and migrants, as illustrated by incidents in Assam, Nagpur, Bihar, and Hyderabad (Weiner, 1978).

The government, which encourages integration (and therefore migration), is drawn into the dilemma of choosing between universalistic and particularistic interests. Because preferential treatment of the local populace is contrary to the universalistic doctrine of rights, it has been government policy to allow migrant minorities to maintain their language and culture within their education system and to demand equality with regard to educational quotas, political representation, and work opportunities. At the same time, the ruling center, afraid to lose local support, has often acted to protect the indigenous population by implementing preferential policies. This has created a dual policy of equal opportunity versus protective discrimination (Weiner, 1978: 343ff). The complexity of the resultant conflict has made it difficult to cope with clashes through purely legal means.

Although internal migration is relatively limited in scope,[1] its repercussions have been strongly felt. This is due to the severity of the problem, as illustrated in the following two cases. (1) An influx of Hindu refugees from Bangladesh over the last thirty years has turned the indigenous population of Tripura into a minority. As no institutional solution has been found to cope with the conflicting demands of the alien majority and the native minority, both of whom demand their constitutional rights, there has been increasing violence between the two groups. (2) Migrants originating from Bangladesh and Bengal who have been attracted to the oilfields of Assam have been the cause of widespread political agitation in that state since early 1980. The Assamian majority has demanded the deportation of the foreigners, who in turn have demanded equal rights. In the meantime riots, protests, and a stoppage or blockage of the flow of petroleum have become almost daily occurrences. The dispute has been further aggravated by its becoming a political issue, with various parties competing for the support of the native voters.

In sum, the accentuation of antagonism in Indian society is due to the institutionalization of social change, increasing fluidity, and a loosening of the boundaries between groups and different codes of conduct.

THE CHANGING NATURE OF MEDIATORY MECHANISMS

In the previous section we argued that discontent, antagonism, and conflicts in India have become more severe in recent years. Nonetheless, most instances of unrest have been handled with the aid of mediatory mechanisms in an institutional or quasi-institutional manner. On the whole there have not been signs of declining legitimacy and integration. This section examines the nature of the mediatory mechanisms used to cope with increasing antagonism.

Morris-Jones has observed that the Indianization of politics has expanded open competition to the point where even the center has to bargain with local forces before it can put decisions into effect (1978:144, 158). It seems that such extended competition has become possible due to three basic developments in the mediatory mechanisms. First, there has been increasing congruence between "objective" and political mechanisms, so that the boundaries between them have become looser. Second, most mediatory processes have been taking place at the local level and not at the center. Third, direct negotiations among equivalent social forces has become the dominant pattern within the mediatory processes.

Due to almost constant electoral processes, the Indian parties and caste associations have increased their mediatory power. In the last national election (January 1980) the parties seem to have become more pluralistic and anchored in the periphery. Mrs. Gandhi won a personal victory, gaining about 43 percent of the votes polled and 67 percent of the Lok Sabha seats, while the Janata Party, in coalition with two smaller parties, gained only about 28 percent (see Table 9:1). Although Mrs. Gandhi was assisted in her campaign by the split between the Ram and Singh factions in the Janata Party and by her charismatic personality, her great success probably stems from her appeal to the elementary needs of the Indian people (calling for an end to poverty and the reinstatement of law and order). Her use of parochial slogans, which legitimated and increased the negotiatory power of small primordial groups and factions, enabled the Congress(I) Party to gain some control over local politics and to somewhat absorb particularistic forces. In this way the party itself operated as a mediatory mechanism between different primordial codes and groups as well as between parochial forces and broader universalistic organizations.

A number of the by-elections held since 1980 have sustained the balance and interchange between local groups and national parties, strengthening the mediatory potential of local branches and caste associations. The national parties have been forced to grant concessions to rural groups in order to gain their support and to create coalitions with different caste associations.

It is, of course, possible to interpret the 1980 Lok Sabha elections and the later by-elections as events in which centripetal processes and the monopoly of the center increased and competition decreased. However, within the Congress Party and other parties, the dominance of the veteran elites has been diminished. An important development has been a rise in the number of what Morris-Jones (1976) calls 'lesser leaders." This phenomenon is not new, but the 1980 elections (probably under the influence of Mrs. Gandhi's late son, Sanjay) accelerated the emergence of young politicians. Having less power than the veterans and relatively few vested interests, they are forced to attend to local demands and to mediate between primordial codes and universal principles. Thus, one may view the 1980 elections and later by-elections as part of a process in which the competition has shifted down to the very

Legitimation and Integration in India

TABLE 9:1

DISTRIBUTION OF LOK SABHA SEATS

1979 and 1980

Party	January 1980	1979 (at dissolution)
Congress(I)	351	80
Congress(U)	13	67
Janata	31	203
Lok Dal	41	77
CPI	11	7
CPM	35	22
DMK	16	...
AIADMK	2	17
Others	19*	29
Independents	6	33
Vacancies	17	7
Total	542	542

* Muslim League 3, National Conference 3, RSP 4, Forward Bloc 3, Akali Dal 1, Maharashtrawadi Gomantak Party 1, Sikkim Janata Parishad 1, Mizoram People's Conference 1, Kerala Congress (Mani group) 1, Kerala Congress (Joseph group) 1.

Source: Data India, January 7–13, 1980, p. 13.

elementary bases of Indian politics. To some extent, this process resembles the one which Tocqueville describes as existing in American democracy, whereby voluntaristic associations link the government with the public (1961:II, 114). In India, caste associations fulfill some of these same functions.

Indian caste associations have become wider in scope, providing support to the political party offering the most benefits. This has increased their mediatory potential in the sense that they can now link different spheres of life and interests.[2] What has further reinforced their mediatory capacity is that the boundaries between class-oriented and primordial affiliations are becoming increasingly ambiguous. The increasing mediatory capacity of caste associations can be exemplified by the case of the harijans.

In India of the 1980s the harijans have aggregated more and more power and have diminished the political gap between themselves and the center of society. Under the leadership of Mr. Ram, himself an untouchable, it has become clear that it is difficult to mobilize their voting power without catering to their interests and thereby improving their bargaining position.

Caste associations have tended to form coalitions with those leaders who are detached from crude caste and regional politics. The fact that these leaders are often relatively unknown, have much fewer vested interests than most other public figures, and hence are ready for an ad hoc coalition has reinforced their mediatory role.

The federal arrangement has also become more mediatory in nature. In each by-election bargaining between the state authorities and the center is resumed and different interests are linked. This process exists in all states, regardless of whether they are dominated by the ruling party.[3]

It is difficult to draw a precise picture of recent developments in "objective" mediatory mechanisms. In general, however, one may observe increasing clashes between two divergent trends. On the one hand, the autonomy of the *panchayat* system, civil administration, legal system, and the press has been strengthened and institutionalized; on the other, this has been countered by constant government attempts to increase its influence over them. Such government influence has been aided by their not being fully differentiated from politics. The struggle between the government and these institutions is unique in that both sides often utilize primordial sentiments to improve their bargaining position, thereby increasing their mediatory power.

The Indian civil administration has been torn between its basic codes and the political pressures exerted by caste associations and representatives.[4] Although it has become more politically oriented, less professional, and perhaps less formal in the last few years (Jain, 1981), it has also become more bureaucratic, impersonal, and universalistic in the running of internal committees, courts, and various mechanisms of control. The clash between particularistic and universalistic codes has created a situation whereby officials have to make many ad hoc decisions. While this has reinforced arbitrariness, it has also increased the administration's expedience and its ability to respond to different interests. The loose boundaries between formal and informal methods have made it less costly to cope with conflicts through the administration than through extra-institutional means.

In recent years the *panchayat rajs* and their *zilla parishads* (district boards) have become more autonomous in their decision-making but more dependent on the center for resources. As they have become important official instruments of policy implementation on the local level, the struggle for dominance over their boards has heightened.[5] The struggle of both local groups and national parties to gain control over the resources allocated by the *panchayat rajs* has led to the mediatory process being utilized at a very elementary local level. The *panchayats* have become flexible tools in the sense that their leadership changes often, in accordance with the political composition of state and/ or national centers. This process can be exemplified by the recent election in Rajastan, where the Congress(I) Party gained full control of the *panchayat* after sixteen years of being in the minority (*The Overseas Hindustan Times*, February 4, 1982:11).

Similarly, the functions of the judicial institutions have become more mediatory in recent years, facilitating the link between center and periphery.

Although there is full constitutional separation between the executive and the judiciary in India (Article 50), there have always been both peaceful exchange and clashes between the two. The executive has accused the judiciary of abusing its power, especially when working to suppress measures intended to promote differential treatment of the weaker social sectors. In reply the judiciary has cited a number of approved acts aimed at promoting the harijans (e.g., the Rent Control Act). For its part, the judiciary has accused the government of interfering with its legal autonomy in order to promote political interests. These clashes have been built into the Indian legal system in several ways. For one, the fact that only 60 percent of the High Court judges are tenured while the remaining 40 percent are temporary enables political manipulation of the judiciary. Although no permanent judge can be removed except by impeachment, any temporary judge can be dismissed upon the completion of his term, regardless of the recommendation of the Chief Justice of India. Hence the government has the power to partially impose its policies on the judiciary. To preserve their autonomy, judges often have no choice but to develop direct relationships with political leaders. This politicization is countered, however, by the legal supervision of the higher courts (see, for example, *Economic and Political Weekly*, July 12–18, 1981: 10–11).

The mediatory power of the court system is further enhanced by internal disagreements regarding governmental intervention and the appointment of judges. One such conflict centered around a government decision not to renew the term of the Delhi High Court judge (S.N. Kumar) after its expiration date in January 1982. This led to a split in the Supreme Court, with some members declaring that the appointment of judges to either the High Court or the Supreme Court should depend not merely on their professional suitability but on other qualities such as honesty and integrity (*The Overseas Hindustan Times*, January 7, 1982:1).

To conclude, the attempt by all three branches of the Indian government – the executive, the legislative, and the judicial – to expand their authority and autonomy has led to constant strains between them. The existence of such conflicts per se has not increased their mediatory power; what is conducive to such power is the overlap of their functions and the intermixing of their codes. As a result of this ongoing process most of the components of the mediatory mechanisms have been strengthened in recent years. This has further loosened the boundaries between political, legal, and administrative institutions. And it is these loose boundaries which have rendered the society both fragile and flexible in its adjustment to different needs, and which have allowed order and disorder to coexist. The operation of mediatory mechanisms has provided Indian society with the means to circumvent antagonism, thereby avoiding paralysis and facilitating the formulation of social priorities and policies.[6]

GENERAL CONCLUSIONS

In most Third World countries the emergence of nationhood has been accompanied by a rise in universalistic, egalitarian expectations which accentuate primordial and class conflicts. Such conflicts, which often pose a threat to political survival, are at times aggravated by the dependency of many of these nations on international markets. Owing to conditions of diversity and poverty, the governments in many developing societies have become dominated by the military. While a regimented government may appear to be a unifying factor in the short run, it often lacks the legitimacy and heterogeneity to absorb all the divisive societal forces. As it is impossible to avoid divisiveness and its accompanying antagonism, the least expensive way to cope with the situation is to institutionalize conflicts within a competitive structure. However, in order for such a framework to function, there is a need for mechanisms capable of mediating between antagonistic codes, sectors, and groups. Such mediatory mechanisms are complex and encompass almost every social sphere, with little differentiation among them; they involve the symmetric relations between equivalent parties which mutually adjust expectations and interests; and their structure is ambiguous, allowing them to serve as an open arena for negotiations.

Mediatory mechanisms function according to a three-phase dialectical pattern: (1) they increase antagonism among different groups and institutions; (2) the balance of power is then stabilized; and (3) the resulting standstill because neither side is able to impose its terms on the other leads to negotiations being held according to universal principles within institutional boundaries. While this process often accentuates the antagonism, the institutional capacity to cope with conflicts is strengthened as a result.

Mediatory institutions have served the interests of the ruling elites not only to maintain their cultural and political dominance but also to integrate the country. The least risky choice has been to slow down social change, converging it somewhat with political change. One of the consequences of this process has been the type of increased economic injustice characteristic of many processes of social change, for example, during the Industrial Revolution in Europe (Moore, 1978). However, this has been mitigated in India by the fact that mediatory mechanisms are used not only by the ruling elites to maintain their privileged position, but also by peripheral groups to obtain some power and mobility. Thus, antagonism and discontent have become incorporated into the system. The very existence of advantages for both groups has reduced political injustice and increased the legitimacy of the Indian system. The result has been gradual, yet stable, social change, in which the most essential codes and institutions are being restructured.[7]

The Indian case provides a sociological model in which conflict and integration have become fused to the point where they even complement one

another. The internal logic of such a social structure is based on an inconsistent paradigm, which creates a high-risk structure whereby order and disorder are easily interchanged. The existence of opposing options enables the
system to absorb its strains and to utilize them for integrative purposes.
Determination of the circumstances under which this type of social structure
declines or flourishes calls for a comparative study of societies with similar
conditions of diversity but different political structures. Such a comparative
study should concentrate not on attempts to integrate conflicting forces but
rather on social mechanisms and elites, which have the potential of absorbing
diversity and promoting social change.

NOTES

1. "According to the 1971 census, while some 30.4 per cent of the population was
enumerated in a locality different from the place of birth, only 3.4 per cent had crossed
the state boundaries, and 1.7 per cent were migrants from outside India. The remaining
25.3 per cent of the population had moved within the state, i.e. was involved in intra-
state migration. A question on the last place of residence also yielded similar estimates of
the number of migrants. In any case, about 76 per cent of the intra-state migrants according to the birth-place criteria (and 78 per cent according to the place of last residence
criteria), were women, moving following their marriage because of a tradition of village
specific exogamy in several parts of India. Most of them move relatively short distances"
(Visaria and Visaria, 1981:1753).

2. In contrast to our approach, Frankel claims: "The net result was that universal
suffrage and an open electoral process by themselves could not create the conditions of
popular pressure from below to accomplish peaceful implementation of social reforms.
Rather, preexisting kinship, caste, and economic ties were projected into vertical patterns
of political mobilization by leaders of the dominant landowning castes to reinforce the
factional structures that divided the poor and prevented them from using their potential
power in superior numbers to pursue common economic interests" (1978:24).

3. In 1980 there were eight states which were not ruled by the Congress(I) Party; six
of them were dominated by a coalition headed by the Janata Party and two by a left-
front coalition.

4. A recent comparative study asserts that the position of bureaucrats in India is
weaker than in countries such as Thailand, where there is direct administrative control
(Kraus et al., 1979:145). This very weakness forces them to serve as mediators between
the center and periphery.

5. Frankel maintains that the *panchayats'* developmental projects often accentuate
conflict between landowners and laborers (1978:189). This in turn motivates the poor
to organize themselves to fight for their own interests. Consequently, their bargaining
power is improved.

6. The fact that the Indian center continues to establish priorities is illustrated by
the 1982 twenty-point program:

"1. Increase irrigation potential, develop and disseminate technologies and inputs
for dry land agriculture.

2. Take special efforts to increase production of pulses and vegetable oil seeds.

3. Strengthen and expand coverage of Integrated Rural Development and
National Rural Employment Programmes.

4. Implement agricultural land ceilings, distribute surplus land and complete
compilation of land records by removing all administrative and legal obstacles.

5. Review and effectively enforce minimum wages for agricultural labour.

6. Rehabilitate bonded labour.

7. Accelerate programmes for the development of Scheduled Castes and Tribes.

8. Supply drinking water to all problem villages.

9. Allot house sites to rural families who are without them and expand programmes for construction assistance to them.

10. Improve the environment of slums, implement programme of house-building for economically weaker sections, and take measures to arrest unwarranted increase in land prices.

11. Maximise power generation, improve the functioning of electricity authorities and electrify all villages.

12. Pursue vigorously programmes of afforestations, social and farm forestry and the development of bio-gas and other alternative energy sources.

13. Promote family planning on a voluntary basis as a people's movement.

14. Substantially augment universal primary health care facilities, and control of leprosy, T.B. and blindness.

15. Accelerate programmes of welfare for women and children and nutrition programmes for pregnant women, nursing mothers and children, specially in tribal, hill and backward areas.

16. Spread universal elementary education for the age group 6–14 with special emphasis on girls, and simultaneously involve students and voluntary agencies in programmes for the removal of adult illiteracy.

17. Expand the public distribution system through more fair price shops, including mobile shops in far-flung areas and shops to cater to industrial workers, students' hostels, and make available to students for text-books and exercise-books on a priority basis and to promote a strong consumer protection movement.

18. Liberalise investment procedures and streamline industrial policies to ensure timely completion of projects. Give handicrafts, handlooms, small and village industries all facilities to grow and to update their technology.

19. Continue strict action against smugglers, hoarders and tax evaders and check black money.

20. Improve the working of the public enterprises by increasing efficiency, capacity utilisation and the generation of internal resources."

(*The Overseas Hindustan Times,* January 28, 1982).

7. Gradual, peaceful change is often perceived as creating structural inconsistencies and divergence and as incapable of coping with rising expectations and injustice (Frankel, 1978). Sudden change, however, may create a gap in legitimacy which reduces stability. Between gradual and sudden change one may find a middle path in which mediatory mechanisms reinterpret common values and institutions and use them to create a legitimate basis for social change.

REFERENCES

Aiyar, S.P. (ed.), 1967. The Politics of Mass Violence in India. Bombay: Manaktalas.

Alatas, S.H., 1968. The Sociology of Corruption. Singapore: Moore Press.

Alexander, K.C., 1968. "Changing religious beliefs and practices of the Rulays of Kerala." Social Action 18 (September—October): 390—398.

Ali, C.M., 1967. The Emergence of Pakistan. New York: Columbia University Press.

Altman, A.A., 1975. "Shinbunshi: The early Meiji adaptation of the Western-style newspaper." Pp. 52—66 in W.G. Beasley (ed.), Modern Japan — Aspects of History Literature and Society. London: Allen and Unwin.

Amin, S., 1977. Imperialism and Unequal Development. Sussex: Harvester Press.

Apter, D., 1961. The Political Kingdom in Uganda. Princeton University Press.

Arora, S.K., 1972. "Social background of the Indian cabinet." Economic and Political Weekly VII, 31—33 (Special Number): 1523—1532.

Awasthy, G.C., 1978. "India." Pp. 197—211 in J.A. Lent (ed.), Broadcasting in Asia and the Pacific. Philadelphia: Temple University Press.

Badhei, S.G. and M.U. Rao, 1968. "Bombay civic election of 1968." Quarterly Journal of Local Self-Government 39 (July—September): 1—20.

Bailey, F.G., 1960. Tribe, Caste and Nation: A Study of Political Activity and Political Change in Highland Orissa. Manchester University Press.

———, 1963. "Closed social stratification in India." Archives Européennes de Sociologie IV, 1:107—124.

Baks, C., 1976. "Dualism and power in municipal administration." Pp. 224—232 in S.D. Pillai (ed.), Aspects of Changing India. Bombay: Popular Prakashan.

Banerjee, S., 1968. National Awakening and the Bangabasi. Calcutta: Amitava-Kalyan.

Bansal, P.L., 1974. Administrative Development in India. New Delhi: Sterling.

Bardhan, P.K., 1974. "The pattern of income distribution in India: A review." Pp. 103—138 in T.N. Srinivisan and P.K. Bardhan (eds.), Poverty and Income Distribution in India. Calcutta: Statistical Publishing Society.

Barnett, S., 1977. "Identity choice and caste ideology in contemporary South India." Pp. 393—414 in K. David (ed.), The New Wind — Changing Identities in South Asia. The Hague: Mouton.

Basu, S., 1975. "Distribution of income among tax-payers." Economic and Political Weekly X, 4:123—127.

Basu, T., 1977. "Calcutta's sandal makers." Economic and Political Weekly XII, 32:1262.

Baum, R.C., 1974. "Beyond convergence: Toward theoretical relevance in quantitative modernization research." Sociological Inquiry 49, 4:225–240.

Baxter, C., 1971. The Jana Sangh; A Biography of an Indian Political Party. Bombay: Oxford University Press.

Beidelman, T.O., 1959. A Comparative Analysis of the Jajmani System. Locust Valley, N.Y.: J.J. Austin.

Bendix, R., 1964. Nation Building and Citizenship; Studies of our Changing Social Order. New York: Wiley.

Benson, J., 1976. "A South Indian jajmani system." Ethnology XVI, 3:239–250.

Berreman, G.D., 1965. "The study of caste ranking in India." Southwestern Journal of Anthropology XXI, 2:115–129.

Beteille, A., 1965. Caste, Class and Power: Changing Patterns of Stratification in a Tanjore Village. Berkeley: University of California Press.

———, 1969. Castes, Old and New. Bombay: Asia Publishing House.

———, 1974. Studies in Agrarian Social Structure. Delhi: Oxford University Press.

Bhagavadgita, 1962. Tr. J. Mascaro. Baltimore: Penguin Books.

Bhagwan, V., 1974. Constitutional History of India and National Movement. Delhi: Atma Ram.

Bhalla, R.P., 1973. Elections in India (1950–1972). New Delhi: S. Chand.

Bhambhri, C.P., 1971. Bureaucracy and Politics in India. Delhi: Vikas.

Bharati, A., 1976. "Sadhuization – An Indian paradigm for political mobilization." Pp. 109–128 in R.I. Crane (ed.), Aspects of Political Mobilization in South Asia. Syracuse University Press.

Bhatt, A., 1975. Caste, Class and Politics. Delhi: Manohar Book Service.

Bhattacharya, J.N., 1896. Hindu Castes and Sects. Calcutta: Thacker, Spink.

Blaug, M., R. Layard and M. Woodhall, 1969. The Causes of Graduate Unemployment in India. London: Allen Lane.

Boeke, J.H., 1953. Economics and Economic Policy of Dual Societies as Exemplified by Indonesia. Haarlem: Tjeenk Willink and Zoon.

Bondurant, J.V., 1958. Regionalism Versus Provincialism: A Study in Problems of Indian National Unity. Berkeley: University of California Press.

Bose, A., 1965. "Six decades of urbanization in India, 1901–1961." The Indian Economic and Social History Review 2 (January): 23–41.

———, 1973. Studies in India's Urbanization, 1901–1971. Bombay: Tata McGraw-Hill.

Braibanti, R., 1963. "Reflections in bureaucratic reform in India." In R. Braibanti and J.J. Spengler (eds.), Administration and Economic Development in India. Durham, N.C.: Duke University Press.

Brass, P.R., 1965. Factional Politics in an Indian State. Berkeley: University of California Press.

———, 1974. Language, Religion and Politics in North India. New York: Cambridge University Press.

Brass, P.R., 1977. "Party systems and government stability in Indian states." The American Political Science Review LXXI, 4:1384–1405.

Brecher, M., 1971. "Elite images and political modernization in India." Pp. 85–102 in A.R. Desai (ed.), Essays on Modernization and Underdeveloped Societies. Vol. II. Bombay: Thacker.

Breman, J., 1974. Patronage and Exploitation: Changing Agrarian Relations in South Gujarat, India. Berkeley: University of California Press.

Broomfield, J.H., 1968. Elite Conflict in a Plural Society: Twentieth Century Bengal. Berkeley: University of California Press.

Brown, J.M., 1972. Gandhi's Rise to Power; Indian Politics 1915–1922. Cambridge University Press.

Brown, W.N., 1966. Man in the Universe; Some Continuities in Indian Thought. Berkeley: University of California Press.

Burke, E., 1955. Reflections on the Revolution in France. New York: Liberal Arts Press.

Burkhart, G., 1975. "Headman and president — Competing strategies of control in a South Indian village." Pp. 61–80 in H.E. Ullrich (ed.), Competition and Modernization in South Asia. New Delhi: Abhinav Publications.

Carras, M.C., 1972. The Dynamics of the Indian Political Factions. Cambridge University Press.

Carter, A., 1974. Elite Politics in Rural India. Cambridge University Press.

Cassen, R.H., 1978. India: Population, Economy, Society. New York: Holmes and Meier.

Cassirer, E., 1955. The Philosophy of Symbolic Forms: Mythical Thought. Vol. II. Tr. R. Manheim. New Haven: Yale University Press.

Chatterjee, B.B., S.S. Singh and D.R. Yadav, 1971. Impact of Social Legislation on Social Change. Calcutta: Minerva Associates.

Chatterjee, G.S., 1976. "Disparities in per capita household consumption in India." Economic and Political Weekly XI, 15:557–567.

Chatterjee, V.B., P.N. Singh and G.R.S. Rao, 1957. Riots in Rourkela: A Psychological Study. New Delhi: Gandhian Institute of Studies.

Chaudhuri, N.C., 1951. The Autobiography of an Unknown Indian. New York: Macmillan.

Chirol, Sir V., 1910. Indian Unrest. London: Macmillan.

Cohn, B.S., 1965. "Anthropological notes on disputes and law in India." Pp. 82–112 in L. Nader (ed.) The Ethnography of Law. American Anthropologist (Special Publication) 67, 6, part 2.

Coleman, J.S. (ed.), 1965. Education and Political Development. Princeton University Press.

Coser, L.A., 1970. Men of Ideas. New York: The Free Press.

Crane, R.I. (ed.), 1976. Aspects of Political Mobilization in South Asia. Syracuse: Maxwell School of Citizenship and Public Affairs.

Cunningham, J.R., 1968 c1941. "Education." In L.S.S. O'Malley (ed.), Modern India and the West. Oxford University Press.

Curran, J.A., 1951. Militant Hinduism in Indian Politics, a Study of the R.S.S. New York: Institute of Pacific Relations.

Dahrendorf, R., 1959. Class and Class Conflict in Industrial Society. Stanford University Press.

Dale, S.F., 1978. Islam and Social Conflict: The Mappilas of Malabar, 1898–1922. Mimeo.

Dalwai, H.U., 1968. Muslim Politics in Secular India. Delhi: Hind Pocket Books.

Dandekar, V.M. and N. Rath, 1971. Poverty in India. Bombay: Indian School of Political Economy. (Reprinted from Economic and Political Weekly VI, November 1 and 2, January 2 and 9, 1971.)

Dasgupta, B., 1974. The Naxalite Movement. Bombay: Allied Publishers.

Dasgupta, B. and R. Laishley, 1975. "Migration from villages." Economic and Political Weekly X, 42:1652–1662.

Dasgupta, B. and W.H. Morris-Jones, 1976. Patterns and Trends in Indian Politics. Bombay: Allied Publishers.

Das Gupta, J., 1970. Language Conflict and National Development: Group Politics and National Language Policy in India. Berkeley: University of California Press.

——, 1981. "India in 1980: Strong center, weak authority." Asian Survey XXI, 2:147–161.

Datta, U., H.D. Chaudhury and P. Narain, 1975. "Current national income statistics: What they tell." Economic and Political Weekly X, 39:1540–1553.

D'Cruz, E., 1967. India, The Quest for Nationhood. Bombay: Lalvani Publishing House.

Derrett, J.D.M., 1979. "Tradition and law in India." Pp. 32–59 in R.J. Moore (ed.), Tradition and Politics in South Asia. New Delhi: Vikas.

Desai, A.R., 1954. Social Background of Indian Nationalism. Bombay: Popular Book Depot.

Desai, M., 1956. The Gita According to Gandhi: Ahmedabad: Navajvan Publishing House.

Desai, M.V., 1977. Communication Policies in India. Paris: UNESCO.

Dhanagare, D.N., 1974. "Social origins of the peasant insurrection in Telangana (1946–1951)." Contributions to Indian Sociology (New Series) VIII:109–134.

——, 1977. "Agrarian conflict, religion and politics: The Moplah rebellions in Malabar in the nineteenth and twentieth centuries." Past and Present (February): 112–141.

Dube, S.C., 1955. Indian Village. London: Routledge and Kegan Paul.

Dubey, S.N., 1973. Organizational Analysis of Panchayati Ray Institutions in India. The Indian Journal of Public Administration XVIII, 2:254–269.

Dubey, S.N. and U. Mathur, 1972. "Welfare programmes for scheduled castes; content and administration." Economic and Political Weekly VII, 4: 165–176.

Dumont, L., 1970 c1966. Homo Hierarchicus. London: Weidenfeld and Nicolson.

Durkheim, E., 1964 c1933. The Division of Labor. Glencoe: The Free Press.

Duverger, M., 1954. Political Parties: Their Organization and Activity in the Modern State. Tr. B. North and R. North. New York: Wiley.

Dwarkadas, R., 1958. Role of Higher Civil Service in India. Bombay: Popular Book Depot.

Eisenstadt, S.N., 1965. Essays in Comparative Institutions. New York: Wiley.

——, 1971. Social Differentiation and Stratification. Glenview: Scott Foresman.

——, 1973. Tradition, Change and Modernity. New York: Wiley.

Eldersveld, S.J. and A. Bashiruddin, 1978. Citizens and Politics. University of Chicago Press.

Eldersveld, S.J., V. Jagannadham and A.P. Barnabas, 1968. The Citizen and the Administrator in a Developing Democracy. New Delhi: Indian Institute of Public Administration.

Embree, A.T., 1972. India's Search for National Identity. New York: Knopf.

Emerson, R., 1960. From Empire to Nation. Cambridge, Mass.: Harvard University Press.

Erdman, H.L., 1967. The Swatantra Party and Indian Conservatism. Cambridge University Press.

Ferrero, G., 1942. The Principles of Power; The Great Political Crises of History. Tr. T.R. Jaeckel. New York: G.P. Putnam's sons.

Field, J.O. and M.F. Franda, 1974. Communist Parties of West Bengal. Cambridge. Mass.: MIT Press.

Fishman, J.A., C.A. Ferguson and J. Das Gupta (eds.), 1968. Language Problems of Developing Nations. New York: Wiley.

Foster, P.J., 1965. Education and Social Change in Ghana. University of Chicago Press.

Fox, R.G., 1969a. "Varna schemes and ideological integration in Indian Society." Comparative Studies in Society and History 11 (January): 27–45.

——, 1969b. From Zamindar to Ballot Box: Community Change in a North Indian Market Town. Ithaca: Cornell University Press.

——, 1970b. "Rajput clans and urban settlements in northern India." In R.G. Fox (ed.), Urban India: Society, Space and Image. Durham, N.C.: Duke University Program in Comparative Studies on Southern Asia.

——, 1971. Kin, Clan, Raja and Rule: Statehinterland Relations in Preindustrial India. Berkeley: University of California Press.

Fox, R.G. (ed.), 1970a. Urban India: Society, Space and Image. Durham, N.C.: Duke University Program in Comparative Studies on Southern Asia.

Franda, M.F., 1971. Radical Politics in West Bengal. Cambridge, Mass.: MIT Press.

Frank, A.G., 1967. Capitalism and Underdevelopment in Latin America. New York: Monthly Review Press.

Frankel, F.R., 1978. India's Political Economy, 1947–1977. Princeton University Press.

Friedmann, Y., 1976. "The Jam'iyyat Al-'Ulamā'-I Hind in the wake of partition." Asian and African Studies XI, 2:181–211.

Friedrich, C.J., 1968. Trends of Federalism in Theory and Practice. London: Pall Mall.

Galanter, M., 1968. "The displacement of traditional law in modern India." The Journal of Social Issues 24 (October): 65–92.

Galanter, M., 1969. "Introduction: The study of the Indian legal profession." Law and Society Review III, 2:201–217.

———, 1971. Secularism and Indian Constitution. Bombay University Press.

———, 1972. "The aborted restoration of 'indigenous' law in India." Comparative Studies in Society and History XIV, 1:53–70.

———, 1979. "Compensatory discrimination in political representation. Economic and Political Weekly XIV, 7 and 8 (Annual Number): 437–452.

Gallagher, J., G. Johnson and A. Seal (eds.), 1973. Locality, Province and Nation: Essays on Indian Politics 1870–1940. Cambridge University Press.

Gandhi, M.K., 1965. To the Students. A.T. Hingorani (ed.), Bombay: Bharatiya Vidya Bhavan.

———, 1968. The Selected Works of Mahatma Gandhi: The Voice of Truth, Vol. IV. S. Narayan (ed.). Ahmedabad: Navajivan Press.

Ganguli, B.N. and D.B. Gupta, 1976. Levels of Living in India. New Delhi: S. Chand.

Gauba, K.L., 1973. Passive Voices: A Penetrating Study of Muslims in India. New Delhi: Sterling.

Gay, P., 1967. The Enlightenment: An Interpretation. London: Weidenfeld and Nicolson.

Geertz, C., 1963. "The integrative revolution: Primordial sentiments and civil politics in the new states." In C. Geertz (ed.), Old Societies and New States. New York: The Free Press.

Ghose Aurobindo, 1937. The Renaissance in India. Calcutta: Arya Publishing House.

———, 1959. The Foundations of Indian Culture. Pondicherry: Sri Aurobindo Ashram.

Ghosh, S., 1975. The Naxalite Movement. Calcutta: Firma K.L. Mukhopadhyay.

Ghouse, M., 1973. Secularism, Society and Law in India. Delhi: Vikas.

Ghurye, G.S., 1968. Social Tensions in India. Bombay: Popular Prakashan.

———, 1969. Caste and Race in India. 5th ed. Bombay: Popular Prakashan.

Gist, N.P. and R.D. Wright, 1973. Marginality and Identity. Leiden: E.J. Brill.

Gould, H.A., 1966. "Religion and politics in a U.P. constituency." Pp. 51–73 in D.E. Smith (ed.), South Asian Politics and Religion. Princeton University Press.

———, 1969. "Toward a jati model of Indian politics." Economic and Political Weekly IV:291–297.

Griffith, J.A.G., 1977. The Politics of the Judiciary. London: Fontana.

Gulliver, P.H., 1973. "Negotiations as a model of dispute settlement: Towards a general model." Law and Society Review 7, 4:667–691.

Gupta, B.S., 1972. Communism in Indian Politics. New York: Columbia University Press.

Gupta, D. 1981. "Caste, infrastructure and superstructure." Economic and Political Weekly XVI, 51:2093–2104.

Gupta, G.R. (ed.), 1978. Cohesion and Conflict in Modern India. New Delhi: Vikas.

Gupta, R.L., 1972. Politics of Commitment: A Study Based on the Fifth General Election in India. New Delhi: Trimurti.

Halayya, M., 1975. Emergency – A War on Corruption. New Delhi: S. Chand.

Hanchett, S., 1976. "Land tenure and social change in a Mysore village." Pp. 181–188 in S.D. Pillai (ed.), Aspects of Changing India. Bombay: Popular Prakashan.

Hanna, W.J. and J.L. Hanna, 1967. "The integrative role of urban Africa's middleplaces and middlemen." Civilizations, XVII: 12–29.

Haqqi, S.A.H., 1967. Union-State Relations in India. Meerut: Meenakshi.

Hardgrave, R.L., 1969. The Nadars of Tamiland: The Political Culture of a Community in Change. Berkeley: University of California Press.

——, 1974. "The Communist parties of Kerala: An electoral profile." In M. Weiner and J.V. Field (eds.), Electoral Politics in the Indian States. Delhi: Manohar Book Service.

——, 1977. "The Mapilla rebellion, 1921: Peasant revolt in Malabar." Modern Asian Studies 11, 1:57–99.

Hardy, P., 1972. The Muslim in British India. Cambridge University Press.

Harrison, S.S., 1960. India: The Most Dangerous Decade. Princeton University Press.

Hartmann, H., 1971. Political Parties in India. Meerut: Meenakshi.

Hechter, M., 1975. Internal Colonialism. London: Routledge and Kegan Paul.

Heesterman, J.C., 1973. "India and the inner conflict of tradition." Daedalus 102,1 (Winter): 97–113.

Hegel, G., 1975. Hegel's Logic. Tr. W. Wallace. Oxford: Clarendon Press.

Heginbotham, S.J., 1975. Cultures in Conflict: The Four Faces of Indian Bureaucracy. New York: Columbia University Press.

Henningham, S., 1981. "Autonomy and organisation." Economic and Political Weekly XVI, 27:1153–1156.

Hoselitz, B.E., 1966. "Interaction between industrial and pre-industrial stratification systems." In N.J. Smelser and S.M. Lipset (eds.), Social Structure and Mobility in Economic Development. Chicago: Aldine.

Husain, S.A., 1961. The National Culture of India. 2nd ed. New York: Asia Publishing House.

Hutton, J.H., 1963 c1946. Caste in India. Bombay: Oxford University Press.

Ilbert, Sir C.P., 1898. The Government of India. Oxford: Clarendon Press.

Inamdar, N.R., 1970. Functioning of Village Panchayats. Bombay: Popular Prakashan.

Irschick, E.F., 1969. Political and Social Conflict in South India; The Non-Brahman Movement and Tamil Separatism, 1916–1929. Berkeley: University of California Press.

Ishwaran, K., 1964. "Customary law in village India." International Journal of Comparative Sociology 5:228–243.

Iyengar, T.S.R., 1974. Center State Relations in India. Prasaranga: University of Mysore.

Jagannadham, V., 1974. "Citizen-administration relationship in development." Pp. 196–215 in V.A.P. Pranandiker (ed.), Development Administration in India. Delhi: Macmillan.

Jagannathan, N.S., 1968. "D.M.K.: The awkward age." Weekend Review 2 (January): 20.

Jain, G.P., 1979. "Mass communication in India." Indian Horizons XXIX, 1:12–16.

Jain, P.C., 1981. Administrative Adjudication: A Comparative Study of France, UK, USA and India. Delhi: Sterling.

Jhangiani, M.A., 1967. Jana Sangh and Swatantra. Bombay: Manaktalas.

Johnson, H.M. (ed.), 1977. "Social system and legal process." Sociological Inquiry 47 (special issue): 3–4.

Joshi, B.R., 1981. "Scheduled caste voters: New data, new questions." Economic and Political Weekly XVI, 33:1357–1362.

Junankar, P.N., 1975. "Green revolution and inequality." Economic and Political Weekly X, 13:A15–A18.

Kahane, R., 1975. "Strategies of legitimizing cultural change: An Indian example." Studies in Comparative International Development 10, 3:88–100.

——, 1981. "Priesthood and social change: The case of the Brahmins." Religion 11:353–366.

——, Higher Education and Elite Formation in India (in preparation).

Kapadia, K.M., 1959. "The family in transition." Sociological Bulletin 8 (September): 68–103.

——, 1966. Marriage and Family in India. 3rd ed. Bombay: Oxford University Press.

Karnik, V.B., 1966. Indian Trade Unions: A Survey. 2nd ed. Bombay: Manaktalas.

——, 1974. Indian Labour: Problems and Prospects; Calcutta: Minerva Associates.

Karnik, V.B. (ed.), 1957. Indian Communist Party Documents 1930–1956. Bombay: Democratic Research Service.

Karve, D.D., 1963. The New Brahmans, Five Maharashtrian Families. Berkeley: University of California Press.

Kessinger, T.G., 1974. Vilyatpur, 1848–1968: Social and Economic Change in a North Indian Village. Berkeley: University of California Press.

Khare, R.S., 1976. Culture and Reality: Essays on the Hindu System of Managing Foods. Simla: Indian Institute of Advanced Study.

Kidder, R.L., 1974. "Formal litigation and professional insecurity: Legal entrepreneurship in South India." Law and Society Review IX, 1:11–37.

Kochanek, S.A., 1968. The Congress Party of India: The Dynamics of One-Party Democracy. Princeton University Press.

Kolenda, P.M., 1963. "Toward a model of the Hindu jajmani system." Human Organization XXII, 1:11–31.

Kolhi, S. (ed.), 1975. Corruption in India. New Delhi: Chetana Publications.

Kopf, D., 1969. British Orientalism and the Bengal Renaissance: The Dynamics of Indian Modernization, 1773–1835. Berkeley: University of California Press.

——, 1974. "The missionary challenge and Brahmo response: Rajnarain Bose and the emerging ideology of cultural nationalism." Contributions to Indian Sociology (New Series) 8:11–24.

Kothari, R., 1970a. Politics in India. Boston: Little, Brown.

———, 1975. Democracy in India: Crisis and Opportunity. Delhi: Allied Publishers.

———, 1976. "End of an era." Seminar (January): 22–28.

Kothari, R. (ed.), 1970b. Caste in Indian Politics. New Delhi: Orient Longman.

Kraus, R., W.E. Maxwell and R.D. Vanneman, 1979. "The interests of bureaucrats: Implications of the Asian experience for recent theories of development." American Journal of Sociology 85, 1:135–155.

Krishnaswami, A., 1964. The Indian Union and the States: A Study in Autonomy and Integration. London: Pergamon.

Kulkarni, M.G., 1976. "Slums in Antangabad City: An ecological approach." Pp. 306–323 in S.D. Pillai (ed.), Aspects of Changing India. Bombay: Popular Prakashan.

Kuper, L., 1971. "Plural societies: Perspectives and problems." Pp. 7–26 in L. Kuper and M.G. Smith (eds.), Pluralism in Africa. Berkeley: University of California Press.

Lal, K.S., 1973. Growth of Muslim Population in Medieval India. Delhi: Research Publication.

Lamb, B.P., 1968 c1963. India: A World in Transition. New York: Praeger.

La Palombara, J., 1974. Politics within Nations. Englewood Cliffs, N.J.: Prentice-Hall.

La Palombara, J. (ed.), 1967 c1963. Bureaucracy and Political Development. Princeton University Press.

Latif, S.A., 1939. The Muslim Problem in India – Together with an Alternative Constitution for India. Bombay: The Times of India Press.

Laxminarayan, H., 1977. "Changing conditions of agricultural labourers." Economic and Political Weekly XII, 43:1817–1820.

Leonard, T.J., 1963. The Federal System of India. Tempe: Bureau of Government Research, Arizona State University.

Lieten, G.K., 1975. "When communism came to India." South Asia 5 (December): 90–100.

———, 1977. "Indian communists look at Indian communism." Economic and Political Weekly XII, 37:1606–1611.

Lipset, S.M. and A. Solari (eds.), 1967. Elites in Latin America. New York: Oxford University Press.

Lokhandwalla, S.T. (ed.), 1971. India and Contemporary Islam. Simla: Indian Institute of Advanced Studies.

Lynch, D.M., 1976. "Some aspects of political mobilization among Adi-Dravidas in Bombay City." Pp. 7-34 in R.I. Crane (ed.), Aspects of Political Mobilization in South Asia. Syracuse University Press.

Madan, T.N. (ed.), 1971. "On the nature of caste in India: A review symposium on Louis Dumont's Homo Hierarchicus." Contributions to Indian Sociology (New Series) v (December): 1–79.

Maddick, H., 1970. Panchayati Raj: A Study of Rural Local Government in India. London: Longman.

Madhok, B., 1970. Indianization? What, Why and How? Delhi: S. Chand.

Maheshwari, B.L., 1973. Center-State Relations in the Seventies. Calcutta: Minerva Associates.

Maine, Sir H.J.S., 1930. Ancient Law. London: John Murray.

Majumdar, R.C., H.C. Raichaudhuri and K. Datta, 1963. An Advanced History of India. Bombay: Macmillan.

Malenbaum, W., 1962. Prospects of Indian Development. Glencoe: The Free Press.

Malik, S.C., 1977. "Indian civilization: New images of the past for a developing nation." Pp. 85–94 in K. David (ed.), The New Wind – Changing Identities in South Asia. The Hague: Mouton.

Mandelbaum, D.G., 1964. "Introduction: Process and structure in South Asian religion." Pp. 5–20 in E.B. Harper (ed.), Religion in South Asia. Seattle: University of Washington Press.

——, 1966. "Transcendental and pragmatic aspects of religion." American Anthropologist 68, 5:1174–1191.

——, 1970. Society in India. 2 vols. Berkeley: University of California Press.

Mankekar, D.R., 1973. The Press Under Pressure. New Delhi: India Book Co.

Mannheim, K., 1940. Man and Society: In an Age of Reconstruction. London: Kegan Paul.

Marriott, M., 1976. "Hindu transactions: Diversity without dualism." Pp. 109–142 in B. Kapferer (ed.), Transaction and Meaning. Philadelphia: ISHI.

Marriott, M. (ed.), 1968 c1955. Village India; Studies in the Little Community. University of Chicago Press.

Mayer, A.C., 1967. "Caste and local politics in India." In P. Mason (ed.), India and Ceylon: Unity and Diversity, a Symposium. Oxford University Press.

Mayhew, L., 1968. "Ascription in modern societies." Sociological Inquiry 38 (Spring): 105–120.

McCully, B.T., 1966 c1940. English Education and the Origin of Indian Nationalism. Gloucester, Mass.: P. Smith.

McKinlay, R.D. and H.S. Cohan, 1975. "Political and economic performance of military and civilian regimes." Comparative Politics 8, 1:1–30.

McLane, J.R., 1977. Indian Nationalism and the Early Congress. Princeton University Press.

Merton, R.K. and E. Barber, 1963. "Sociological ambivalence." Pp. 91–120 in E.A. Tiryakian (ed.), Sociological Theory, Values and Socio-cultural Change. New York: The Free Press.

Meyer, J.W., J. Boli-Bennett and C. Chase-Dann, 1975. "Convergence and divergence in development." Annual Review of Sociology 1:223–245.

Miller, D.B., 1975. From Hierarchy to Stratification: Changing Patterns of Social Inequality in a North Indian Village. Delhi: Oxford University Press.

Miller, R.E., 1976. Mappila Muslims of Kerala. Bombay: Orient Longman.

Misra, B.B., 1970. Administrative History of India 1834–1947. Bombay: Oxford University Press.

——, 1976. The Indian Political Parties: An Historical Analysis of Political Behaviour up to 1947. Delhi: Oxford University Press.

Monteiro, J.B., 1966. Corruption, Control of Maladministration. Bombay: Manaktalas.

Moore, B., 1966. Social Origins of Dictatorship and Democracy. Boston: Beacon Press.

——, 1978. Injustice: The Bases of Obedience and Revolt. London: Macmillan.

Morris-Jones, W.H. (ed.), 1976. The Making of Politicians: Studies from Africa and Asia. London: Athlone Press.

——, 1978. Politics Mainly Indian. Bombay: Orient Longman.

Morrison, C., 1974. "Clerks and clients: Paraprofessional roles and cultural identities in India litigation." Law and Society Review, 9, 1:39–62.

Mukherjee, M. and G.S. Chatterjee, 1974. "Growth of national income in India since independence." Economic Affairs XIX, 6–7:251–266.

Muller, M., 1966 c1910. The Sacred Books. New Delhi: Motilal Banarsidass.

Myrdal, G., 1968. Asian Drama: An Inquiry into the Poverty of Nations. 3 vols. New York:Pantheon.

Narain, D. (ed.), 1975. Explorations in the Family and Other Essays. Bombay: Thacker.

Narain, I. (ed.), 1976. State Politics in India. Meerut: Meenakshi.

Narain, P., 1970c 1968. Press and Politics in India, 1885–1905. Delhi: Munshiram Manoharlal.

Narayan, J.P., 1970. Communitarian Society and the Panchayati Rai. Brahmanand (ed.), Varanasi: Navachetna Prakastan.

Nash, M., 1964. "Southeast Asian society: Dual or multiple?" The Journal of Asian Studies 23 (May): 417–423.

Natarajan, S., 1962. A History of the Press in India. Bombay: Asia Publishing House.

Nehru, J., 1949. Independence and After. Delhi: Publications Division, Ministry of Information and Broadcasting, Government of India.

Nicholson, N.K., 1968. "India, modernizing faction and the mobilization of Power." International Journal of Comparative Sociology 9 (December): 302–317.

Nigam, R.C., 1971. Language Handbook on Mother Tongues in Census: Census Centenary Monograph 10. Census of India 1971, Annexure 1, LI–LVI.

Nimkoff, M.F., 1959. "The family in India: Some problems concerning research on the changing family in India." Sociological Bulletin 8 (September): 32–38.

Nonet, P. and P. Selznick, 1978. Law and Society in Transition. Towards Responsive Law. New York: Harper and Row.

Ojha, P.D. and V.V. Bhatt, 1964. "Patterns of income distribution in an underdeveloped economy." The American Economic Review 54 (September): 711–720.

O'Malley, L.S.S., 1974 c1932. Indian Caste Customs. London: Curzon Press.

Omvedt, G., 1976. Cultural Revolt in a Colonial Society: The Non-Brahmin Movement in Western India 1873–1930. Bombay: Scientific Socialist Education Trust.

Oommen, T.K., 1971. Charisma Stability and Change: An Analysis of the Bhoodon Oramdan Movement in India. New Delhi: Thomson Press.

Oommen, T.K., 1975. "Agrarian legislation and movements as sources of change; the case of Kerala." Economic and Political Weekly X, 40: 1571–1584.

——, 1977. "Analyzing rural social change: A perspective." Pp. 83–100 in M.N. Srinivas, S. Seshaiah and V.S. Parthasarathy (eds.), Dimensions of Social Change in India. Bombay: Allied.

Oren, S., 1973. "Caste, religion and parties in Kerala 1956–1970." Asian Profile 1, 2:329–344.

Orwell, G., 1963. Burmese Days. New York: Signet.

Ostrogorski, M., 1902. Democracy and the Organization of Political Parties. 2 vols. Tr. F. Clarke. New York: Macmillan.

Overstreet, G.D. and M. Windmiller, 1959. Communism in India. Berkeley: University of California Press.

Palmer, N.D., 1975. "The crisis of democracy in India." Orbis XIX, 2:379.

Panikkar, K.M., 1963. The Foundations of New India. London: Allen and Unwin.

Pareto, V., 1935. The Mind and Society. 4 vols. London: J. Cape.

Park, R.E., 1928. "Human migration and the marginal man." American Journal of Sociology 33 (May): 881–893.

Park, R.L., 1967. India's Political System. Englewood Cliffs, N.J.: Prentice-Hall.

——, 1975. "Political crisis in India, 1975." Asian Survey XV, 11:996.

Parkin, F., 1968. Middle Class Radicalism; The Social Bases of the British Campaign for Nuclear Disarmament. New York: Praeger.

Parsons, T., 1964. Essays in Sociological Theory. New York: The Free Press.

Patil, S., 1979. "Dialectics of caste and class conflicts." Economic and Political Weekly XIV, 7 and 8 (Annual Number): 287–296.

Patnaik, U., 1976. "Class differentiation within the peasantry." Economic and Political Weekly XI, 39:A82–A101.

Peaslee, A.J., 1974. Constitution of Nations – Asia, Australia and Oceania. Vol. II, rev. 3rd ed. The Hague: Martinus Nijhoff.

Potter, D.C., 1966. "Bureaucratic change in India." In R. Braibanti (ed.), Asian Bureaucratic Systems Emergent from British Imperial Tradition. Durham, N.C.: Duke University Press.

Prakash, K., 1973. Language and Nationality: Politics in India. Bombay: Orient Longman.

Prasad, G.K., 1974. Bureaucracy in India. New Delhi: Sterling.

Premi, K.K., 1974. "Educational opportunities for the scheduled castes." Economic and Political Weekly IX, 45 and 46:1902–1910.

Press, I., 1969. "Ambiguity and innovation: Implications for the genesis of the cultural broker." American Anthropologist 71 (April): 205–217.

Pye, L.W., 1958. "Administrators, agitators and brokers." In D. Lerner and A.J. Wiener (eds.), Attitude Research in Modernizing Areas. Public Opinion Quarterly 22 (Fall): 342–348.

Radhakrishnan, S., 1974 c1939. Eastern Religions and Western Thought. Oxford University Press.

Raghaviah, Y., 1968. "The dichotomy of specialists and generalists in Panchayati Raj pattern of Andhra Pradesh." Quarterly Journal of the Local Self-Government 38 (April-June).

Rai, Lala Lajpat, 1920. The Problem of National Education in India. London: Allen and Unwin.

———, 1966. Writing and Speeches. 2 vols. V.C. Hoshi (ed.). Delhi: University Publishers.

———, 1967. A History of the Arya Samaj. Calcutta: Orient Longman.

Rajon, M.S., 1969. "The impact of British rule in India." Journal of Contemporary History 4 (January): 89–102.

Ram, M., 1968. Hindi Against India; the Meaning of D.M.K. New Delhi: Rachna Prakashan.

Ramaswamy, U., 1974. "Self-identity among scheduled castes: A study of Andhra." Economic and Political Weekly IX, 47:1959–1964.

Ranga, N.G., 1949. Revolutionary Peasants. New Delhi: Amrit Book Co.

Rangaswami Iyengar, A., 1933. The Newspaper Press in India. Bangalore City: Bangalore Press.

Rao, K.S., 1973. "Role of the judiciary in Indian democracy." In K.S. Rao et al., Judiciary and Social Change. Bangalore City: The Ecumenical Christian Center.

Rao, M.S.A., 1970. Urbanization and Social Change. New Delhi: Orient Longman.

———, 1977. "Rewari kingdom and Mughal empire." Pp. 79–89 in R.G. Fox (ed.), Realm and Religion in Traditional India. Durham, N.C.: Duke University Program in Comparative Studies on Southern Asia.

Rao, M.S.A. (ed.), 1974. Urban Sociology in India. New Delhi: Orient Longman.

Rao, V.K.R.V., 1979. "Changing structure of Indian economy." Economic and Political Weekly XIV, 59:2049–2058.

Rao, V.M., 1981. "Nature of rural underdevelopment." Economic and Political Weekly XVI, 41:1655–1666.

Rastogi, P.N., 1975. The Nature and Dynamics of Factional Conflict. Delhi: Macmillan.

Ray, S., 1978. Freedom Movement and Indian Muslims. New Delhi: People's Publishing House.

Reddy, K.N., 1975. "Inter-state tax effort." Economic and Political Weekly X, 50:1916–1924.

———, 1976. "Inter-state difference in social consumption." Economic and Political Weekly XI, 24:872–879.

Reddy, M.P., 1969. "Indian student rebellion, some neglected factors." Economic and Political Weekly IV, 15:357–360.

Reeves, P., 1976. "Pathways to political advancement: Problems of choice for Taluqdar politicians in late British India." Pp. 103–115 in W.H. Morris-Jones (ed.), The Making of Politicians: Studies from Africa and Asia. London: Athlone Press.

Riggs, F.W., 1964. Administration in Developing Countries. Boston: Houghton, Mifflin.

Robinson, F., 1974. Separatism Among Indian Muslims. Cambridge University Press.

Rosen, G., 1966. Democracy and Economic Change in India. Berkeley: University of California Press.

Rosenthal, D.B., 1976. The City in Indian Politics. Faridabad: Thomson Press.

Rothermund, D., 1979. "Traditionalism and national solidarity in India." Pp. 191–197 in R.J. Moore (ed.), Tradition and Politics in South Asia. New Delhi: Vikas.

Rowe, P., 1969. "Indian lawyers and political modernization: Observations in four district towns." Law and Society Review III, 2:219–250.

Roy, A.K., 1975. The Spring Thunder and After: A Survey of the Maoist and Ultra-Leftist Movements in India 1962–1975. Calcutta: Minerva Associates.

Roy, N.C., 1958. The Civil Service in India. Calcutta: K.L. Mukhopadhyay.

Roy, R., 1970. "Caste and political recruitment in Bihar." Pp. 228–258 in R. Kothari (ed.), Caste in Indian Politics. New Delhi: Orient Longman.

Roy, Raja Rammohun, 1906. English Works by R.R.M. Roy. Allahabad.

——, 1962. Life and Letters of R.R. Roy (compiled by S.D. Collet). Calcutta.

Rudolph, L.I. and S.H. Rudolph, 1967. The Modernity of Tradition: Political Development in India. University of Chicago Press.

Saberwal, S., 1976. Mobile Men: Limits to Social Change in Urban Punjab. New Delhi: Vikas.

Santhanam, K.I., 1960. Union-State Relations in India. Bombay: Asia Publishing House.

Saraswathi, S., 1974. Minorities in Madras State. Delhi: Impex India.

Sarkar, C., 1967. The Changing Press. Bombay: Popular Prakashan.

Sarkar, S., 1972. The Center and the States. Calcutta: Academic Publications.

Sartori, G., 1966. "European political parties: The case of polarized pluralism." In J. La Palombara and M. Weiner (eds.), Political Parties and Political Development. Princeton University Press.

——, 1976. Parties and Party Systems. Cambridge University Press.

Schumpeter, J.A., 1950. Capitalism, Socialism and Democracy. 3rd ed. New York: Harper.

Schutz, A. and T. Luckmann, 1974. The Structures of the Life-World. Tr. R.M. Zaner and H.T. Englehardt. London: Heinemann.

Scott, J.C., 1969. "The analysis of corruption in developing nations." Comparative Studies in Society and History 11 (June): 315–341.

——, 1976. The Moral Economy of the Peasant: Rebellion and Subsistence in Southeast Asia. New Haven: Yale University Press.

Seal, A., 1968. The Emergence of Indian Nationalism: Competition and Collaboration in the Later Nineteenth Century. Cambridge University Press.

Seidman, R.B., 1972. "Law and development: A general model." Law and Society Review 6, 3:311–342.

Selznick, P., 1969. Law, Society and Industrial Justice. New York: Russell Sage Foundation.

Seminar, 1969. A Selection of Articles on Nationhood (March).

——, 1974. The Indian Muslims: A Symposium on the Attitudes of a Major Minority (February).

——, 1975. Symposium on the Need for Rational Policy (May).

Sen, A., 1975. Employment, Technology and Development. Oxford: Clarendon Press.

Sen, L.K., 1969. Opinion Leadership in India. Hyderabad: National Institute of Community Development.

Sen, L.K., V.R. Gaikward and G.L. Varma, 1967. People's Image of Community Development and Panchayati Raj. Hyderabad: National Institute of Community Development.

Sen, S., 1977. Working Class of India: History of Emergence and Movement 1830–1970. Calcutta: Bagchi.

Senart, E., 1975. Caste in India. Tr. Sir E. Denison Ross. Delhi: Ess Ess Publications.

Setalvad, M.C., 1975. Union and State Relations Under the Indian Constitution. Calcutta: Eastern Law House.

Shah, A.B., 1967. Planning for Democracy and Other Essays. Bombay: Manaktalas.

Sharif, J., 1972 c1921. Islam in India. Tr. G.A. Hemklots. London: Curzon Press.

Sharma, G.B., 1975. "Law as an instrument for abolition of untouchability; case of Rajasthan." Economic and Political Weekly X, 15:635–641.

Sharma, G.K., 1971. Labour Movement in India. New Delhi: Sterling.

Sharma, P.D., 1975. "Law and order administration: Some basic issues." In N.K. Seth and J.C. Kukkar (eds.), Administration of Law and Order. Jaipur: Indian Institute of Public Administration.

Sheth, D.L., 1975. "Structure of Indian radicalism." Economic and Political Weekly X, 56 and 57 (Annual number): 319–334.

Sheth, T.N., 1960. "A note on the unity of India." Sociological Bulletin 9 (March): 37–45.

Shils, E., 1961. The Intellectual between Tradition and Modernity: The Indian Situation. The Hague: Mouton.

——, 1966. "The intellectuals in the political development of the new states." In J.L. Finkle and R.W. Gable (eds.), Political Development and Social Change. New York: Wiley.

——, 1975. Center and Periphery. University of Chicago Press.

Singer, M., 1972. When a Great Tradition Modernizes. An Anthropological Approach to Indian Civilization. New York: Praeger.

Singh, A., 1973. Leadership Patterns and Village Structure: A Study of Six Indian Villages. New Delhi: Sterling.

Singh, B., 1961. Next Step in Village India: A Study of Land Reform and Group Dynamics. London: Asia Publishing House.

Singh, V., 1973. "The changing pattern of social stratification in India." Pp. 137–154 in M.N. Srinivas, S. Seshaiah, and V.S. Parthasarathy (eds.), Dimensions of Social Change in India. Bombay: Allied.

Sinha, A., 1977. "Murder of a peasant leader." Economic and Political Weekly XII, 31:1214–1215.

Sinha, V.K. (ed.), 1969. Secularism in India. Bombay: Lalvani Publishing House.

Smelser, N.J., 1962. Theory of Collective Behavior. New York: The Free Press.

Smelser, N.J., 1968. Essays in Sociological Explanation. Englewood Cliffs, N.J.: Prentice-Hall.

——, 1971. "Stability, instability and the analysis of political corruption." In B. Barber and A. Inkeles (eds.), Stability and Social Change. Boston: Little, Brown.

Smith, D.E., 1958. Nehru and Democracy: The Political Thought of an Asian Democrat. Bombay: Orient Longman.

——, 1963. India as a Secular State. Princeton University Press.

Sovani, N.V., 1965. "British impact on India." Pp. 110–176 in G.S. Metraux and F. Crouzet (eds.), The New Asia. New York: Mentor.

Spear, P., 1965. A History of India. Vol. II. London: Penguin Books.

Sreenivasan, K., 1964. Productivity and Social Environment. New York: Asia Publishing House.

Srinivas, M.N., 1962. Caste in Modern India. Bombay: Asia Publishing House.

——, 1969. Social Change in Modern India. Berkeley: University of California Press.

Srivastava, G.N., 1970. The Language Controversy and the Minorities. Delhi: Atma Ram.

Srivastava, R.C., 1971. Development of Judicial System in India under the East India Company from 1833 to 1858. Lucknow Publishing House.

Stockes, E., 1976. "Return of the peasant to South Asian history." South Asia 6 (December): 96–111.

Stonequist, E.V., 1964. "The marginal man: A study in personality and culture conflict." In E.W. Burgess and D.J. Bogue (eds.), Contributions to Urban Sociology. Chicago: University of Chicago Press.

Sundarayya, P., 1972. The Telengana People's Struggle and Its Lessons. Calcutta: Desraj Chadh (on behalf of the Marxist Communist Party of India).

Tandon, P., 1968 c1961. Punjabi Century 1857–1957. Berkeley: University of California Press.

Tangri, S.S., 1960. "Intellectuals and society in the nineteenth century India." Comparative Studies in Society and History 3:368–394.

Tape, T.K., 1967. "Protective discrimination and educational planning." In G.S. Sharma (ed.), Educational Planning: Its Legal and Constitutional Implications in India. Bombay: The Indian Law Institute.

Taub, R.P., 1969. Bureaucrats Under Stress: Administrators and Administration in an Indian State. Berkeley: University of California Press.

Tilak, B.G., 1935 c1915. Om Tat-Sat Srimad Bhagavagita Rahasya or Karma Voga Sastra. Tr. B.S. Sukthankar (Vol. I, 1935; Vol. II, 1936). Poona: Tilak Bros.

Tilman, R.O., 1963. "The influence of caste on Indian economic development." Pp. 202–223 in R. Braibanti and J. Spengler (eds.), Administration and Economic Development in India. Durham, N.C.: Duke University Press.

Tinker, H., 1966. "Structure of the British imperial heritage." in R. Braibanti (ed.), Asian Bureaucratic Systems Emergent from British Imperial Tradition. Durham, N.C.: Duke University Press.

Tocqueville, A. de, 1961. Democracy in America. New York: Vintage.

Trivedi, H.R., 1976. Urbanism: A New Outlook. Delhi: Atma Ram.

Umapathy, M., 1968. "Emerging power pattern in India." Indian Journal of Political Science 39:197–203.

Vajpeyi, D.K., 1977. "Performance in Uttar Pradesh and its impact on social change and modernization, 1966–1976." The Indian Journal of Public Administration XXIII, 4:940–969.

Varkey, O., 1974. At the Crossroads: The Sino-Indian Border Dispute and the Communist Party of India, 1959–1963. Calcutta: Minerva Associates.

Vepa, R.K., 1967. "Civil servants: Are they a breed apart?" The Indian Journal of Public Administration 8:227–234.

Visaria, P. and L. Visaria, 1981. "Indian population scene after the 1981 census: A perspective." Economic and Political Weekly XVI, 44, 45, 46: 1727–1780.

Vyas, V.S. and S.C. Bandyopadhyay, 1975. "National food policy in the framework of a national food budget." Economic and Political Weekly X, 13:A2–A13.

Walch, J., 1976. "Party system in Tamil Nadu: The institutionalization of cleavages." Pp. 101–119 in S.D. Pillai (ed.), Aspects of Changing India. Bombay: Popular Prakashan.

Weber, M., 1947. The Theory of Social and Economic Organization. New York: The Free Press.

——, 1954. Max Weber on Law in Economy and Society. Cambridge, Mass.: Harvard University Press.

——, 1958. The Religion of India. New York: The Free Press.

Weiner, M., 1965. "India: Two political cultures." In L.W. Pye and S. Verba (eds.), Political Culture and Political Development. Princeton University Press.

——, 1967. Party Building in a New Nation. The Indian National Congress. University of Chicago Press.

——, 1976. "India's new political institution." Asian Survey XVI, 9:898–901.

——, 1978. Sons of the Soil. Princeton University Press.

Weiner, M. (ed.), 1975. Electoral Politics in India. Three States: Three Disadvantaged Sectors. Columbia, Mo.: South Asian Books.

Weintraub, D., 1970. "Rural periphery, societal center and their interaction in the process of agrarian development: A comparative analytical framework." Rural Sociology 35, 3:367–376.

Westergaard, K., H.S. Muller and K. Nyholm, 1976. "Livestock adoption and small farmers." Pp. 153–162 in S.D. Pillai (ed.), Aspects of Changing India. Bombay: Popular Prakashan.

Wiser, W.H. and C.M. Wiser, 1971. Behind Mud Walls, 1930–1960. Berkeley: University of California Press.

Wolf, E.R., 1973. Peasant Wars of the Twentieth Century. London: Faber and Faber.

Yadav, R.K., 1969. The Indian Language Problem. Delhi: National Publishing House.

Zagoria, D.S., 1971. "The ecology of peasant Communism in India." American Political Science Review 65, 1:144–160.

Official and Semi-Official Sources of Pre-Independence British India and the Indian Union

PRE-INDEPENDENCE BRITISH INDIA

Census of India, for the years 1911, 1921, 1931, 1941.
Statistical Abstract for British India, for the periods 1911/12 – 1920/21 to 1929/30 – 1938/39. Delhi: Manager of Publications.
Report of the Calcutta University Commission (Sadler Report). Calcutta Parliamentary Papers, Vol. 14, 1919.
Review of Growth of Education in British India by the Auxiliary Committee Appointed by the Indian Statutory Commission (Hartog Report). London, 1929.
Report of the Indian Statutory Commission (Sir John Allsebrook Simon Commission), Vols. I–III. Calcutta: Government of India Central Publication Branch, 1930.

THE INDIAN UNION

Statistical Abstract of the Indian Union, for various years over the period 1949–1972. Delhi: Statistical Organization Department of Statistics, Cabinet Secretariat.
Report of the University Education Commission, 1948/49 (Radhakrishnan Report), 2 vols. New Delhi: Ministry of Education, 1950.
Census of India, for the years 1951, 1961, 1971.
Report of the Press Commission, Pt. I. New Delhi: Ministry of Information and Broadcasting, 1954.
The First Five Year Plan (a draft outline). Delhi: Government of India Planning Commission, 1952.
Report of the Press Commission, Comments on Reaction. New Delhi: Lokh Sabah Secretariat, 1955.
Report of the Official Language Commission, 1956. Delhi: Government of India, 1957.
Reports of the Committees of the Panel on Land Reform, 1956. Delhi: Government of India Planning Commission, 1958.
Report of the Seminar on National Integration. New Delhi: University Grants Commission, 1958.
Report on the Pattern of Graduate Employment fof the years 1960, 1961, 1963. New Delhi: Ministry of Labour and Employment, Directorate General of Employment and Training.
Report of the Commission on Emotional Integration. New Delhi: Ministry of Education, 1962.
Report of the Committee on Reservation for Backward Classes in the Services. Maharashtra: General Administration Department, 1962.
Report of the Commissioner for Linguistic Minorities. New Delhi: Ministry of Home Affairs. Eighth report, 1965/66.
Report of the Education Commission, 1964–1966. New Delhi: Ministry of Education, 1966.

AICE, All India Colloquium on Ethical and Spiritual Values as the Basis of National Integration. Bombay: Ramakrishnan Executive. Records of Proceedings, December 30, 1966 – January 2, 1967.

Report of the National Integration Council and Unit, Summary Record of the First Meeting of the N.I.C. New Delhi: Ministry of Home Affairs, October 26, 1968.

Report of the National Integration Council and Unit, Summary Record of the Second Meeting of the Standing Committee of the Council. New Delhi: Ministry of Home Affairs, March 20, 1969.

Bulletin of the National Integration Unit, No. 12/5/69. New Delhi: Ministry of Home Affairs, April 30, 1969.

Report of the Committee of Experts on Unemployment Estimates. Delhi: Planning Commission, 1970.

University Grants Commission Report for the Year 1970/71. New Delhi, 1973.

Economic Growth and Income Distribution. Bangkok: United Nations Economic Commission for Asia and the Far East, 1971.

Press in India, 1972, Pt. I: Sixteenth Report of the Registrar of Newspapers for India Under Press and Registration of Books Act. New Delhi: Ministry of Information and Broadcasting, 1973.

Report of the Committee on Unemployment (B. Bhagavati Report). New Delhi: Ministry of Labour and Rehabilitation, Department of Labour and Employment, 1973.

Constitution of India. New Delhi: Ministry of Information and Broadcasting, 1973 (rev. ed.).

Draft Five Year Plan, 1978–1983. New Delhi: Government of Indian Planning Commission, 1978.

INDEX

Akali Dal 59, 65
Anand Marg 14, 67, 101
Antagonism xi-xiii, 1, 55, 91, 111, 113
  changing patterns of 106, 108
  political 10
  sources of 21-22
  structural 1, 3, 76
  (see also Antagonistic codes, principles;
    Legitimation, antagonistic patterns
    of)
Antagonistic codes, principles xi, 5-6,
  20, 28-29, 32, 47, 75-76
  bridging of xii, 7, 47, 65, 75-76, 79-
    80, 113
  institutionalization of 55, 65, 78, 113
  (see also Duality, structural)
Anti-Brahmin Movement 27, 61, 66
Arya Samaj 50

Bargaining
  arena 6, 68-69, 77, 79, 81, 94
  devices 71
  political 31, 68, 70, 74, 81, 111
  power 38, 65, 73, 114
Bengal 23, 30, 45, 62, 77, 108
Beteille, A. 23, 72, 86
Bhagavadgita 40-41, 47
Bharatya Lok Dal (BLD) 76, 103
Bhatt, A. 22-23
Brahma Samaj 50
Brahminization 72
Brahmins 23, 35, 37, 46, 50, 54, 66, 71
Bridging mechanisms (see Mediatory
  mechanisms)
British colonial system 34, 39, 53, 80,
  88
Brown, J.M. 52-53
Brown, W.N. 36, 84

Caste(s) 15-16, 22-26, 107
  boundaries between 38, 85
  coalitions of 23, 25
  differences between 9, 16-17, 31, 36

lower 13, 22-23, 27, 35-36, 46, 61-
  62, 66, 82
middle 46, 62
scheduled 22, 35, 46, 62, 67, 73
structure of xii, 13
system 37, 61, 64, 82, 86
upper 13, 23, 35, 37, 39-40, 50, 73,
  82
Caste associations 20, 23, 69-73,
  109-111
  and the legal system 82-83
  as mediatory mechanisms 55, 69-71,
    109-111
  as political forces 27, 70-73, 77, 110
Center 10, 59, 63, 66-68, 73-74, 84,
  109, 111
  and periphery, gap between 2, 20, 29,
    53, 73, 79
  connection to periphery 50, 59, 67,
    74, 84
  ruling 34, 100, 108
  (see also Periphery)
Chanans (see Nadars)
Chirol, Sir V. 24
Class(es)
  conflicts between xi, 2, 12, 21-22, 24,
    31, 64, 76, 77, 113
  divisions 2, 6, 8, 21-25, 31, 82, 106
  interests 14, 16, 21, 24, 31, 58, 61-63,
    65, 84
  lower 17, 19, 21, 39, 46, 63, 65, 100,
    106-107
  middle 21, 40, 44, 59, 63, 65, 100,
    106-107
  upper 21, 40, 44, 59, 63, 65, 100,
    106-107
Communication 56, 92
  mass media of 43, 56, 78-79, 92-94,
    96, 98, 103, 111
  censorship of 98, 102-103
  radio 93
  the press 79, 93-94, 96, 98, 111
  traditional networks of 92

137